A Singer's Companion

TO THE CHURCH YEAR

Cycle C

A Singer's Companion

TO THE CHURCH YEAR

Lawrence J. Johnson

The Pastoral Press
Washington, DC

ISBN: 1-56929-022-9

The Pastoral Press
225 Sheridan Street, NW
Washington, DC 20011

The Pastoral Press is the publications division of the National Association of Pastoral Musicians, a membership organization of musicians and clergy dedicated to fostering the art of musical liturgy.

Printed in the United States of America.

To
Marlene and Marisa

INTRODUCTION

The initial liturgical reforms implemented as the fruit of Vatican II resulted in hard times for many choirs. The introduction of the vernacular rendered obsolete much of the past repertoire. Focus on the role of the assembly's song appeared to weaken the function of the choir. Directors and members were challenged to re-vision themselves and their role within the liturgical celebration.

Happily (yet not without a certain modicum of pain) the challenge has been met. Choirs are alive and well in most parish communities. There is enthusiasm, dedication, and loyalty. A highly diversified repertoire is developing. Diocesan choir festivals and workshops are becoming more frequent. Choir directors are increasingly acquiring liturgical and musical skills.

This book is intended to further the diocesan and parish efforts presently being undertaken to support the role of the choir. It does so by promoting the musical, liturgical, and spiritual growth of all who, through the art of choral song, assist and support the assembly's sung prayer.

Jeremiah 33:14-16   Psalm 25:4-5, 8-9, 10, 14
1 Thessalonians 3:12-4:2   Luke 21:25-28, 34-36

To you, O Lord, I lift my soul.

Make me to know your ways, O Lord;
   teach me your paths.
Lead me in your truth and teach me,
   for you are the God my salvation;
   and for you I wait all day long.

Good and upright is the Lord;
   therefore he instructs sinners in the way.
He leads the humble in what is right,
   and teaches the humble his way.

All the paths of the Lord are steadfast love and faithfulness,
   for those who keep his covenant and his decrees.
The friendship of the Lord is with those who fear him,
   and he makes his covenant known to them.

Psalm 25, an alphabetic psalm where each couplet begins with the next letter of the Hebrew alphabet, is a prayer for guidance and forgiveness. The text speaks of a God who is a forgiving God, a God who "leads the humble to what is right," a God who is good and upright, kind and constant. And this is why the whole assembly can join in the refrain "To you, O Lord, I lift my soul."

This psalm well captures the spirit of Advent, which is a time of watching, preparation, and waiting: "for you I wait all day long."

FOR THE JOURNEY

During Advent the church waits not only for the approaching feast of Christmas but also, and more importantly, for the glorious coming of Christ at the end of time.

Waiting is also an important part of preparing choral prayer. Both singers and director have to wait. Waiting till the music arrives from the publisher, waiting till the music is learned (being patient, for example, while the tenors learn their part), waiting till the particular liturgical occasion when the music is sung. Waiting is an integral part of our preparation.

As singers and directors we are always looking toward tomorrow—we are always in a state of waiting. And it is through patience and prayer that we support one another as we wait, that we assist one another in our common ministry of serving the prayer of God's people.

ADVENT

Beginning with the 4th and 5th centuries Christians in various localities felt a need to set aside special weeks to prepare for Christmas (just as they had been doing for Easter by means of Lent), either by special fasts or by special prayers. Rome did the latter by the end of the 6th century.

In time this Advent (the word means "coming") took on a highly penitential character: the Alleluia was not sung on weekdays, the Gloria was omitted, the ministers wore violet vestments, the organ was silenced. The 3rd Sunday of Advent was considered to be a respite from penance: it was called *Gaudete* Sunday: rose vestments were worn; there was organ music, etc.

Today Advent no longer has a special penitential character: it is a time of awaiting and preparing for Christmas and for Christ's Second Coming at the end of time. It is a period of devout prayer and joyful expectation.

PRAYER

All-powerful God,
with joy and anticipation
we await the coming of Christ your Son.
Prepare our minds and hearts
so that with constant hope
we may always sing
the songs of your kingdom.

"The Advent mystery is then a mystery of emptiness, of poverty, of limitation. It must be so. Otherwise it could not be a mystery of hope." Thomas Merton, *Seasons of Celebration*, 1965.

Baruch 5:1-9   Psalm 126:1-2, 2-3, 4-5, 6
Philippians 1:4-6, 8-11   Luke 3:1-6

R. *The Lord has done great things for us; we are filled with joy.*

When the Lord restored the fortunes of Zion,
  we were like those who dream.
Then our mouth was filled with laughter,
  and our tongue with shouts of joy.

Then it was said among the nations,
  "The Lord has done great things for them."
The Lord has done great things for us,
  and we rejoiced.

Restore our fortunes, O Lord,
  like the watercourses in the Negeb.
May those that sow in tears
  reap with shouts of joy.

Those who go out weeping,
  bearing the seed for sowing,
shall come home with shouts of joy,
  carrying their sheaves.

Psalm 126 prays for the restoration of the Jewish homeland. The psalmist's song is a joyful plea that God lead the people out of captivity. There is a sense of urgency here: the Lord is to restore the people's fortunes "like the watercourses in the Negeb," namely, suddenly; during summer the riverbeds are dry till a rain turns them into a sudden torrent of water.

This psalm magnificently complements today's first reading from the prophet Baruch who prophecies that the captivity of the Jewish people in Babylon will soon end. The works of the Lord are indeed a reason for rejoicing; they are the reason "we are filled with joy."

FOR THE JOURNEY

As singers, all of us have our personal mountains to be made low; we have valleys to be filled in (see today's first reading).

4

There is always one or another obstacle hindering the musical service we give to the members of our community.

For some it may be a particular style of music, or perhaps the music of a particular composer or music from a particular histori-cal period. All too often we are held captive by our musical prejudices.

And yet God's beauty can be heard everywhere ... but only if we allow our hearts and ears to be open to God's Spirit.

"O" ANTIPHONS

Among the most beautiful treasures of the church are the "O" Antiphons, a set of 7 texts sung to Gregorian Chant and used before and after the *Magnificat* (the Canticle of Mary) at Evening Prayer (Vespers) from December 17th to 23rd.

The name derives from the initial "O" of the text, which uses ancient biblical images to present the divine titles of the incarnate Word. Here is the first antiphon:

"O Wisdom, you came forth from the Mouth of the Most High, and reaching from the beginning to end, you ordered all things mightily and sweetly. Come, and teach us the way of prudence."

These texts—their author is unknown—were sung in the Roman Church as long ago as the time of Charlemagne (8th century). In cathedrals, monasteries, and other religious communities the singing was often accompanied by special ceremonies (incense, smoke, candles, etc.).

PRAYER

Lord, our God,
we look forward to the coming of your Son.
Teach us to discover you in all that is good.
Open our hearts
so that we may find your song
in every corner of creation.

"But all of you as individuals should become a choir so that, sounding together in harmony, singing the song of God in unison, you may with one voice sing praise to the Father through Jesus Christ, that he may hear you." Ignatius of Antioch (d.c. 107).

5

Zephaniah 3:14-18   Isaiah 12:2-3, 4, 5-6
Philippians 4:4-7   Luke 3:10-18

R. *Cry out with joy and gladness:*
     for among you is the great and Holy One of Israel.

Surely God is my salvation;
     I will trust, and will not be afraid,
for the Lord God is my strength and my might;
     he has become my salvation.
With joy you will draw water
     from the wells of salvation.

Give thanks to the Lord, call on his name;
     make known his deeds among the nations;
     proclaim that his name is exalted.

Sing praise to the Lord, for he has done gloriously;
     let this be known in all the earth.
Shout aloud and sing for joy, O royal Zion,
     for great in your midst is the Holy One of Israel.

The responsorial psalm for today is taken from Isaiah. The author utters praise and thanksgiving because of the wondrous deeds wrought by God.

This joyful psalm continues the exuberance of the first reading from Zephaniah who says that "the Lord is in your midst," a thought echoed by Isaiah's "for great in your midst is the Holy One of Israel." The Lord is always present and is always yet to come.

FOR THE JOURNEY

Discouragement afflicts all of us . . . in various ways and at different times. Yes, even in our choral ministry.

Over and over again we practice an extremely difficult passage, and all to no avail. We re-hearse a particular selection till it is perfect, only to have the unexpected happen when the piece is sung during the liturgy.

Yet the words of Zephaniah hold true: "Be not discouraged." The motive? As St. Paul says in today's reading: "God's own peace . . . will stand guard over your hearts and minds."

If we only allow God to take charge of our song, we will be at peace no matter what occurs.

_____ "O" ANTIPHONS (continued) _____

Here is the opening text of each of the "O" Antiphons:

Dec.

17   O Wisdom, O Holy Word of God (*O Sapientia*)
18   O Sacred Lord of Ancient Israel (*O Adonai*)
19   O Flower of Jesse's Stem (*O Radix Jesse*)
20   O Key of David (*O Clavis David*)
21   O Radiant Dawn (*O Oriens*)
22   O King of all the Nations (*O Rex gentium*)
23   O Emmanuel (*O Emmanuel*)

Notice that the titles given to Jesus in the Latin, when read backwards, form an acrostic: *Ero cras* = "I will be tomorrow"—an allusion to Christmas eve.

Our popular *Veni, Veni, Emmanuel* is a (9th century?) metrical version of the "O" Antiphons with a tune (perhaps of medieval French origin) different from that used in monasteries.

PRAYER

Father in heaven,
you give us the gift of peace,
the peace that can be found
only in Jesus Christ your Son.
Sustain us
as we raise our voices
in proclaiming the joy of salvation.

"The success of congregational singing depends, of course, on the personal exertions of the pastor. Without his leadership and steady cooperation, all the efforts of the people would be wasted. A zeal that is timid, faint-hearted, and spasmodic will not suffice. The rector should throw all the weight of his energies into the work." John Cardinal Gibbons, Archbishop of Baltimore, *The Ambassador of Christ* (1896).

Micah 5:1-4   Psalm 80:1-2, 14-15, 17-18
Hebrews 10:5-10   Luke 1:39-45

R. *Lord, make us turn to you,*
  let us see your face and we shall be saved.

Give ear, O Shepherd of Israel,
  you who are enthroned upon the cherubim,
    shine forth.
Stir up your might,
  and come to save us.

Turn again, O God of hosts;
  look down from heaven, and see;
have regard for this vine,
  the stock that your right hand has planted.

But let your hand be upon the one at your right hand,
  the one whom you made strong for yourself.
Then we will never turn back from you;
  give us life, and we will call on your name.

The psalmist implores the Lord's help for Israel. The whole land, and especially the north, lies in ruins. Samaria, the northern Kingdom, was overrun in 721 B.C.; pagan immigrants inhabit the land—they are like so many weeds inhibiting the growth of the vine. And thus the prophet cries out for help.

In today's first reading Micah speaks of the Messiah as one who will "shepherd his flock," the same image with which the psalmist begins: "Give ear, O Shepherd of Israel." The Messiah is not only a shepherd but also a king, namely, "the one at your right hand."

FOR THE JOURNEY

This last week before Christmas is often one of increased activity for singers and musicians—with additional and longer rehearsals. New pieces to polish...old selections to refresh ...all kinds of last minute details. The Christmas season is second only to the Easter Triduum in what is musically required of us.

And so it is with all the more reason that we should use this week to seek out short periods of quiet, peace, and calmness.

We need time to be alone with ourselves, with Jesus the Lord, and with the Spirit dwelling within us. Having rested awhile in quiet prayer, we—refreshed—can energetically sing of Christ the Lord whose birth we recall on Christmas Day.

CAROL

The Christmas season is a time for carols, which are popular and traditional songs usually having the events of this season as their theme. And yet there are also carols for Easter, springtime, etc.

The term "carol" comes from the Old French word *carole* (a "round dance") and perhaps indicates the far distant origins of such traditional songs.

Compared to hymns, carols are of a more popular nature; they are less dogmatic. Carol singing at Christmas became popular in England during the mid-nineteenth century.

PRAYER

All-powerful God,
help us find
moments alone with you,
so that nourished by your presence
we might truly rejoice in song
as we celebrate Christ's coming
among us.

"It is unfortunate that we are more inhibited (and less faithful to the Gospels) than our medieval ancestors, whose statues of Mary often portray her as pregnant. There is something to be said for that kind of blunt iconography. Pregnancy isn't a very comfortable thing. Its hope is tinged with nausea and awkwardness and anxiety. You can't see the face of the one who is to come. And that is what Advent is about." Ralph Keifer, *New Catholic World* (1979).

Isaiah 9:1-6   Psalm 96:1-2, 2-3, 11-12, 12-13
Titus 2:11-14   Luke 2:1-14

R. *Today is born our Savior, Christ the Lord.*

O sing to the Lord a new song;
    sing to the Lord, all the earth.
Sing to the Lord, bless his name.

Tell of his salvation from day to day.
Declare his glory among the nations,
    his wondrous works among all the peoples.

Let the heavens be glad, and let the earth rejoice;
    let the sea roar, and all that fills it;
    let the field exult, and everything in it.
Then shall all the trees of the forest sing for joy before
        the Lord.

For he is coming, for he is coming to judge the earth.
He will judge the world with righteousness,
    and the peoples with his truth.

Psalm 96, which appears in somewhat altered form in 1 Chronicles 16:23-33, is a hymn of joy celebrating the kingship of Yahweh. It is an act of hope—the future belongs to the God who reigns over all.

The first reading, from Isaiah, speaks of God's vast and peaceful "dominion," God's kingdom, a theme echoed by the psalmist who speaks of the Lord who "is coming to judge the earth."

FOR THE JOURNEY

Christmas is about many wonderful things: family, carols, decorated trees, cribs, a festive meal, not to mention gift-giving; we exchange gifts as we remember that Christ is God's gift to us, that Christ is God dwelling among us.

Human gifts usually come enclosed in wrappings, and unwrapping the present is part of the joy of receiving it.

Music itself is a gift from God, and we—often by discipline and dedication—unwrap that gift as our voices transform a printed page of notes into sounds of praise and thanksgiving. How impoverished our lives would be if there were no gift of music! And how poorer our worship would be!

THE CRIB

No symbol is more closely associated with Christmas than the crib. The origins of representing Christ's Nativity by means of a crib (from the Latin *corbis*, meaning a "basket") or a manger (from the French *manger* ["to eat"], here a trough in a stable) is generally ascribed to St. Francis of Assisi who in 1223 "staged" a living tableau of the Nativity.

The personages depicted usually are those found in the various gospel accounts; yet historically there is a tendency to multiply the people who come to pay their respects to the infant Jesus; for example, in some areas of France fishermen, hunters, poachers, and others all appear in the scene.

And should you visit Rome ... the reputed remains of Christ's crib are preserved at the basilica of St. Mary Major.

PRAYER

Father of all goodness,
you give us the gift of your Son.
Help us to share Christ with others
through the gift of music and song.
Fill us with joy
so that we might be
true heralds of the Gospel.

"God sent His singers upon the earth
With songs of sadness and of mirth,
That they might touch the hearts of men
And bring them back to heaven again."

Henry Wadsworth Longfellow (1807-1882)

11

Numbers 6:22-27   Psalm 67:1-2, 4, 5, 7
Galatians 4:4-7   Luke 2:16-21

R. *May God bless us in his mercy.*

May God be gracious to us and bless us
   and make his face to shine upon us,
that your way may be known upon earth
   your saving power among all nations.

Let the nations be glad and sing for joy,
   for your judge the peoples with equity
   and guide the nations upon the earth.

Let the peoples praise you, O God;
   let all the peoples praise you.
May God continue to bless us;
   let all the ends of the earth revere him.

Psalm 67 invites the *whole* world to praise God—truly an "ecumenical psalm." People everywhere are called upon to give thanks to God who is requested to "bless" them, namely, to extend divine favor upon them.

The psalmist speaks of God's countenance shining upon us—a figure of speech found in today's first reading which contains the priestly or Aaronic blessing. All people—being blessed by God—can, in turn, worship God.

FOR THE JOURNEY

Today's feast—and it is the most ancient Marian observance—celebrates Mary as the Mother of God. Spiritual writers often remind us that Mary was an example of constant and trusting prayer.

We have often heard that our liturgical celebrations are to be prayerful celebrations where all participating raise their voices in praise and supplication, celebrations in which we encounter God Our Creator and Redeemer.

And yet we also needs moments of prayer alone. As individuals we need to find a time and a space for our own personal prayer . . . before the liturgy. As someone once said, if we cannot pray to God outside the liturgy, we will have a hard time doing so within the liturgy.

LITURGY

The word "liturgy" is a commonly used word among Catholics today to designate the celebration of the Mass, the sacraments, the liturgy of the hours. The term has its origins in the classical Greek word *leitourgia*, namely, a work (*érgon*) undertaken on behalf of all the people.

In the Greek Old Testament the word was a technical term for worship; and in Hebrews 8:2 it is used to designate Christ's priestly ministry.

By the 4th century the word "liturgy" was applied by the eastern church to the eucharistic celebration. It was only in the 16th century that the Latin *liturgia* started to become accepted in the west as a general term referring to the whole worship activity of the church. The term reminds us that worship is something *all of us do together*. It is a communal activity.

PRAYER

All-powerful God,
may we, like Mary,
experience the joy of singing your
praises.
May she be our model of prayer,
of love, and of service.

"A well-trained choir adds beauty and solemnity to the liturgy and also assists and encourages the singing of the congregation. The Second Vatican Council, speaking of the choir, stated emphatically: 'Choirs must be diligently promoted,' provided that 'the whole body of the faithful may be able to contribute that active participation which is rightly theirs'." Bishops' Committee on the Liturgy, *Music in Catholic Worship* (1972) no. 36.

Isaiah 60:1-6   Psalm 72:1-2, 7-8, 10-11, 12-13
Ephesians 3:2-3, 5-6   Matthew 2:1-12

> R. *Lord, every nation on earth will adore you.*
>
> Give the king your justice, O God,
>   and your righteousness to a king's son.
> May he judge your people with righteousness,
>   and your poor with justice.
>
> In his days may righteousness flourish
>   and peace abound, until the moon is no more.
> May he have dominion from sea to sea,
>   and from the River to the ends of the earth.
>
> May the kings of Tarshish and of the isles
>   render him tribute,
> may the kings of Sheba and Seba
>   bring gifts.
>
> For he delivers the needy when they call
>   the poor and those who have no helper.
> He has pity on the weak and the needy
>   and saves the lives of the needy.

This psalm, perhaps composed for the coronation of a Jewish king, also glorifies an ideal king who for Christians is Christ the Lord. The psalmist speaks of kings from afar (Tarshish = the far west [?]; Seba = Ethiopia [?]) coming and bearing gifts.

The psalm mirrors today's first reading, from Isaiah, which tells of the wealth of nations being brought from distant places, e.g., Sheba, to the little city Jerusalem.

FOR THE JOURNEY

From the earliest centuries of Christianity the Magi have appealed to the popular religious imagination (the wise men from the east are depicted in the early second century-cemetery of St. Priscilla at Rome).

The gifts offered by the Magi have today been replaced by the offering of our very selves to

14

Christ, especially as this offering is represented by the bread and wine for the eucharist.

Part of this self-giving is found in our gift of song. And yet this gift requires more than technical perfection, as important as technique is. If our song is to be a true gift, it must spring forth from loving and faithful hearts.

_____ RITE _____

A word that occurs quite frequently with liturgical connotations is "rite," from the Latin *ritus*, meaning a "custom" or a "usage." The word has several meanings. For example:
• the totality of actions and words used during a particular liturgical function (e.g., the rite of baptism);
• individual elements in such a totality (e.g., the rite of pouring water);
• the liturgical tradition, practices, and spiritualities of particular churches (e.g., the Roman rite, the Byzantine rite, etc.)

PRAYER

Most loving Father,
you have enriched us with the
gift of your Son.
May the melodies of our song
reflect the many riches you have
given us.
Help us to recognize Christ's
sanctifying presence
among us.

"At times the choir, within the congregation of the faithful and as a part of it, will assume the role of leadership, while at other times it will retain its own distinctive ministry. This means that the choir will lead the people in sung prayer, by alternating or reinforcing the sacred song of the congregation, or by enhancing it with the addition of a musical elaboration. At other times in the course of liturgical celebration the choir alone will sing works whose musical demands enlist and challenge its competence." Bishops' Committee on the Liturgy, *Music in Catholic Worship* (1972) no. 36.

Isaiah 62:1-5   Psalm 96:1-2, 2-3, 7-8, 9-10
1 Corinthians 12:4-11   John 2:1-12

R. *Proclaim his marvelous deeds to all the nations.*

O sing to the Lord a new song;
    sing to the Lord, all the earth.
Sing to the Lord, bless his name.

Tell of his salvation from day to day.
Declare his glory among the nations,
    his marvelous works among all the peoples.

Ascribe to the Lord, O families of the peoples,
    ascribe to the Lord glory and strength.
Ascribe to the Lord the glory due his name.

Worship the Lord in holy splendor;
    tremble before him all the earth.
Say among the nations, "The Lord is king!
    He will judge the peoples with equity."

This psalm, also used at Midnight Mass on Christmas, is a song of joyful praise.

In today's first reading the prophet Isaiah tells of the future vindication of Jerusalem: "The nations shall see your vindication . . . For as a young man marries a young woman, so shall your builder marry you" (the account of the marriage at Cana occurs in today's gospel). God will indeed carry out the divine plan for our salvation. It is for this reason that the psalmist calls upon the people to "proclaim [God's] marvelous deeds to all the nations."

Our God is indeed a faithful God. God's promises will be fulfilled—even today. For this we too give thanks.

FOR THE JOURNEY

The psalmist tells us to "sing to the Lord a new song." Each time we sing, even if it is a piece we have sung hundreds of times previously, we are indeed singing a "new song."

There is a special uniqueness about music for, unlike the plastic arts, music is always new, always being created afresh at a particular moment.

As singers we, as it were, constantly share in God's creation. We are singularly privileged and blessed, for our ministry is to create beauty which will inspire and energize new rhythms of prayer in the people we serve.

ORDINARY TIME

Today we begin what is known as Ordinary Time, namely that part of the liturgical year having no distinctive emphasis as we find in, for example, Advent, Lent, the Easter Season.

Ordinary Time, which lasts 34 weeks, begins on the Monday after the Sunday following January 6 and continues till the Tuesday before Ash Wednesday; the season resumes on the Monday after Pentecost Sunday and continues till the beginning of Advent.

On the Sundays of Ordinary Time we celebrate the mystery of Christ in all its fullness, without any further specification.

One author has written that the Sundays of Ordinary Time "represent the ideal Christian Sunday . . . the Lord's Day in its pure state as presented to us in the Church's tradition" (P. Jounel).

PRAYER

Father of heaven and earth,
your work of creation continues
through human hands and voices.
Help us so that the music we make
may be inspired
by the beauty and power of your
holy name.

" . . . we want a liturgy that transforms the heart of the people of God into burning love for the Lord. We also want singing that raises the people's prayer on the wings of beauty, art, and inspiration." Consilium, *Letter to Bishop Charrière of Fribourg* (21 August 1965).

Nehemiah 8:2-4, 5-6, 8-10   Psalm 19:7, 8, 9, 14
1 Corinthians 12:12-30 or 12:12-14, 27   Luke 1:1-4; 4:14-21

R. *Your words, Lord, are spirit and life.*

The law of the Lord is perfect,
    reviving the soul;
the decrees of the Lord are sure,
    making wise the simple.

The precepts of the Lord are right,
    rejoicing the heart;
the commandment of the Lord is clear,
    enlightening the eyes.

The fear of the Lord is pure,
    enduring forever;
the ordinances of the Lord are true
    and righteous altogether.

Let the words of my mouth and the meditation of
        my heart
    be acceptable to you.
O Lord, my rock and my redeemer.

This psalm is a peaceful reflection in praise of God's law (namely, the Torah) which the psalmist also calls God's decree, precept, command, and ordinances.

The law is God's word ("Your words, Lord, are spirit and life") and today both the first reading and the gospel tell us of the people hearing the proclamation of God's word.

FOR THE JOURNEY

Words are important to singers, and especially important to Christian singers.

When we sing, we bring together—we unite—text and music so that a new entity comes into existence. The sung word takes on a new dimension, a dimension that transcends ordinary speech. Through music the word can penetrate, enliven, and inspire hearts with the power of God's grace.

But for this to happen, God's

word must first reach and transform our own hearts. In short, we must be converted.

We must constantly strive toward holiness; we must turn away from selfishness and sin toward the God who is the source of all beauty and good. We do this by hearing the Scriptures, by meditating—praying on the Scriptures, and—with the support of others—by reorienting our lives, indeed our very existence, to God.

As Christians, we are constantly being converted by God's written word. As Christian singers, we are proclaimers of both words and of Christ who is the Word.

CHOIR/CHORUS

All of us are members of a "choir," and some of us might also be members of a "chorus." Both terms are used to designate a vocal ensemble composed of a larger number of singers with more than one person taking a part. Both words come from the Greek *choros* (a band of dancers and / or singers).

In popular usage the term "choir" refers to a body of singers who ordinarily perform "religious" music. (The word "choir" is also applied to instrumental groups within the orchestra, e.g., the brass choir, the string choir).

The word "chorus" is a more general term, although usually it refers to a group of singers whose repertoire is customarily more "secular" in character.

When two complete bodies of singers are used, we have what is known as a "double chorus" or a "double choir."

PRAYER

Loving Father,
you have sent us your Word
so that we might
follow the way of truth and
freedom.
Give us the strength
to live by the words we sing.

"The Holy Spirit prays in the Liturgy and when we pray with the Liturgy the Holy Ghost, the Spirit of Christ, prays in us. He teaches us how to pray by praying in us ... He not only gives us words to say and sing, He also sings them in our hearts." Thomas Merton, *Bread in the Wilderness*, 1960.

Jeremiah 1:4-5, 17-19   Psalm 71:1-2, 3-4, 5-6, 15-17
1 Corinthians 12:31-13:13 or 13:4-13   Luke 4:21-30

R. *I will sing of your salvation.*

I you, O Lord, I take refuge;
    let me never be put to shame.
In your righteousness deliver me and rescue me;
    incline your ear to me and save me.

Be to me a rock of refuge,
    a strong fortress, to save me.
    for you are my rock and my fortress.
Rescue me, O my God, from the hand of the
    wicked.

For you, O Lord, are my hope,
    my trust, O Lord, from my youth.
    it was you who took me from my mother's
    womb.

My mouth will tell of your righteous acts,
    of your deeds of salvation all day long,
O God, from my youth you have taught me,
    and I still proclaim your wondrous deeds.

Psalm 71 is the song of an aged psalmist (see verse 9) who has always trusted in God and continues to do so. The author has spent a lifetime of service and now God is closer than ever.

The first reading tells of God calling the young Jeremiah. Both the psalmist and the prophet responded, as youths, to God's call to serve.

FOR THE JOURNEY

Paul in this Sunday's reading speaks of love, love that never fails, love that is patient, enduring . . . For the Christian the foundation of such love is union with Christ. Through baptism we have become one with Christ and one with each other.

Many parishes are fortunate enough to benefit from the ministries of several choral groups—there might be, for example, the "adult" choir, the "contemporary" choir, and the children's choir. In addition there are cantors, organists, and other instrumentalists.

Yet all of us share in *one* music ministry, just as all of us share in the one body of Christ. Each group complements another. We are all servants of the one Christ. Musical diversity, yet ministerial unity.

THE SCHOLA

In the Roman Catholic Church one of the traditional designations for the choir is the Latin word "*schola*." The use of this word goes back to an ancient "school" of boy choristers located in Rome.

We know very little about this early music school. One legend claims that Pope Sylvester (314-335) was its founder. Another legend attributes its establishment to Pope Leo I (440-461). What is certain is that during the early Middle Ages cantors or teachers from such a school in Rome were sent to various centers of western Christendom where other such singing schools were founded. The schola—seen as an extension of the clergy—was officially restricted to men and boys.

The word "*schola*" is only infrequently applied to the choir today, and yet the term reminds us that our work as singers requires constant learning and growth, both in terms of music and in terms of service.

PRAYER

Lord God,
you are the source of unity and love.
Help all the singers of this
community
to be united in their service
to others and to one another.
Help them to be one
in heart, in mind,
and in love.

"Why should the devil have all the good tunes?" Rowland Hill (1744-1833), *Sermons*.

Isaiah 6:1-2, 3-8   Psalm 138:1-2, 2-3, 4-5, 7-8
1 Corinthians 15:1-11 or 15:3-8, 11   Luke 5:1-11

R. *In the sight of the angels*
   I will sing your praises, Lord.

I give you thanks, O Lord, with my whole heart;
   before the gods I sing your praise;
I bow down toward your holy temple
   and give thanks to your name.

For your steadfast love and your faithfulness;
   for you have exalted your name and your word
      above everything.
On the day I called, you answered me,
   you increased my strength of soul.

All the kings of the earth shall praise you, O Lord,
   for they have heard the words of your
      mouth.
They shall sing of the ways of the Lord,
   for great is the glory of the Lord.

Though I walk in the midst of trouble,
   you preserve me against the wrath of my
      enemies;
you stretch out your hand,
   and your right hand delivers me.

This psalm thanks God for having heard the psalmist's prayer and invites the mighty ones of the earth to join in a hymn of praise, a hymn sung both in heaven and on earth.

The angels of Psalm 138 recall the seraphim (literally, those "burning ones") who appear in the vision of Isaiah where they also utter praise to the Lord.

FOR THE JOURNEY

Angels appear frequently in both the Old and New Testaments. They are the "heavenly court," guardians of persons and places, mediators and messengers, companions of Christ, etc.

22

In today's selection from the Book of Revelation the author speaks of these heavenly beings as offering praise to "the Lamb who was slain."

The tradition of the church, especially the church of the east, has long suggested that the choir represents the angels. Thus in the Byzantine Liturgy, at the entrance, the choir alone sings "We who mystically represent the *cherubim*..." In a special way our song on earth reflects the song of the angels in heaven.

Our earthly liturgy mirrors that of heaven.

HYMN

Hymn singing is an important part of our Christian heritage and of our service as choir members. The term "hymn" comes from the Greek "*hymnos*," meaning a "song of praise."

The early church used this word to designate a variety of religious compositions, some of which were included in the Bible itself. But in time the word was restricted to newly written compositions, as distinguished from scriptural pieces.

One of the characteristics of hymnody is that a hymn comprises several stanzas or verses witten in a recurring meter.

St. Hilary (d.366) is usually credited with having written the first hymn in Latin. But since almost all of his hymns have been lost, St. Ambrose might be more properly called the father of hymnody.

The Eastern Churches give hymnody a more prominent place in the liturgy than does the Roman Church.

PRAYER

God of mercy and love,
you have created all things
in heaven and upon earth.
Hear our prayers during this
season of resurrection joy.
May our melody become one
with that of the angels above.

"Above, the hosts of angels sing praise; below, men form choirs in the churches ... the inhabitants of heaven and earth are brought together in a common solemn assembly; there is one thanksgiving, one shout of joy, one joyful chorus." John Chrysostom (c.347-407).

Sixth Sunday of the Year   February 12, 1995

Jeremiah 17:5-8   Psalm 1:1-2, 3, 4, 6
1 Corinthians 15:12, 16-20   Luke 6:17, 20-26

R. *Happy are they who hope in the Lord.*

Happy are those
    who do not follow the advice of the wicked,
or take the path that sinners tread,
    or sit in the seat of scoffers;
but their delight is in the law of the Lord,
    and on his law they meditate day and night.

They are like trees planted by streams of water,
    which yield their fruit in its season
    and their leaves do not wither.
In all that they do, they prosper.

The wicked are not so,
    but are like chaff that the wind drives away.
For the Lord watches over the way of the righteous,
    but the way of the wicked will perish.

Psalm 1 outlines the "way," namely, the manner of living followed by the good and the wicked. As the first piece in the Book of Psalms, this composition sets the stage for the whole collection.

Today's readings are about trust, hope, and confidence: Jeremiah contrasts the good and the wicked; Jesus blesses those whose only hope is in God; and Paul tells us that Christ's resurrection is the foundation of our hope. Those who hope and trust in God will find happiness indeed.

FOR THE JOURNEY

Proper intonation, rhythmic exactness, correct enunciation, choral blend—in fact, all the elements that come together to form a choir's skill—are essential for a choir's success and for its members to experience a sense of artistic accomplishment.

Yet of itself technical excellence does not guarantee the presence of prayer, and prayer is, after all, the reason we gather for common worship. Nonetheless, the quality of the music we make is of great consequence. Artistic excellence can move—can free—

24

the human spirit so that it might more easily respond in prayer to the ever-present promptings of the Holy Spirit. True art is a bearer of the spiritual.

Just as a tree needs nourishment, sunlight, and careful pruning if it is to bear fruit, the same is true for the musical sounds we make. Through practice, through rehearsal we perfect our vocal craft, not to garner applause, but to better serve the gathered people and their prayer.

TUNE METERS

If you look at your parish hymnal you will notice that various letters (e.g., L.M. or S.M.) or numbers (e.g., 6.6.11.D) appear in conjunction with each hymn; these are called tune meters and indicate the number of lines in each verse and the number of syllables in each line.

For example, common meter (C.M.) has four lines, the first and third lines having eight syllables, and the second and fourth lines having six syllables (8.6.8.6)).

> O God, our help in ages past,
> Our hope for years to come,
> Our shelter from the stormy blast,
> And our eternal home.

Indicating tune meters *helps* match a hymn text to a tune of the same meter.

PRAYER

All powerful God,
we place our trust in you.
Look kindly upon us
and help us
so that our song be a pleasing song,
one whose beauty and grace
inspire true prayer.

"Pray with moderation and calm, and chant psalms with understanding and proper measure, and you will be raised on high like a young eagle." Evagrius Ponticus (346-349).

1 Samuel 26:2, 7-9, 12-13, 22-23   Psalm 103:1-2, 3-4, 8, 10, 12-13
1 Corinthians 15:45-49   Luke 6:27-38

R. *The Lord is kind and merciful.*

Bless the Lord, O my soul,
  and all that is within me,
    bless his holy name.
Bless the Lord, O my soul,
  and do not forget all his benefits.

Who forgives all your iniquity,
  who heals all your diseases,
who redeems your life from the Pit,
  who crowns you with steadfast love and mercy.

The Lord is merciful and gracious,
  slow to anger and abounding in steadfast love.
He will not always accuse,
  nor will he keep his anger forever.

As far as the east is from the west
  so far he removes our transgressions from us.
As a father has compassion for his children,
  so the Lord has compassion for those who fear
    him.

This hymn of praise and thanksgiving begins with the psalmist talking to himself. The motive here is that God has been kind to both the psalmist and the nation.

Compassion is required by Our Lord in today's gospel; and the first reading provides us with an example of David showing compassion. So we praise the Lord who "crowns us with compassion," who "has compassion on those who fear him."

FOR THE JOURNEY

The message of Jesus is one of change, of radical change or conversion (as today's gospel illustrates). We are constantly called

26

to alter the direction of our lives. We are to refocus our attention from the things of this world to those of heaven.

In a way, constant change is characteristic of the Christian singer: how often we are required to learn a new composition, to modify the way we render a well-known piece, to alter the way we sing a certain musical passage, perhaps to modify the way we understand our role in the parish's ministry of music

The manner whereby we respond to this demand for change says much about how we understand our role as servants of the community's song, since every community is also in a constant state of change, always moving forward in its journey of faith.

NAME THAT TUNE

Since hymn texts can, at least in theory, be sung to any number of melodies or tunes, the practice has developed of assigning "tune names" to these melodies. This custom supplies an easy way of identifying a melody without singing or humming its initial notes.

Hymn tune names come from a variety of sources; most frequently the tunes are given saints' names (St. Theodulph), the names of cities (Moscow), and original first lines ("Lasst uns erfreuen").

PRAYER

God of all mercy,
you call us to transform our lives
so that we may attain the joys of
your kingdom.
By the power of your grace
may our song be the fruit
of truly converted hearts.

"See that what you sing with your mouth
You believe with your heart.
And that what you believe in your heart
You obey in your works."
John of Salisbury (c.1115-1180).

Sirach 27:4-7   Psalm 92:1-2, 12-13, 14-15
1 Corinthians 15:54-58   Luke 6:39-45

R. *Lord, it is good to give thanks to you.*

It is good to give thanks to the Lord,
    to sing praises to your name, O Most High;
to declare your steadfast love in the morning
    and your faithfulness by night.

The righteous flourish like the palm tree,
    and grow like a cedar in Lebanon.
They are planted in the house of the Lord;
    they flourish in the courts of our God.

In old age they still produce fruit;
    they are always green and full of sap,
showing that the Lord is upright;
    he is my rock, and there is not unrighteousness
        in him.

According to its title in the Bible, this psalm was said in the synagogue on the morning of the Sabbath. It is a hymn extolling the just deeds of God. Because of the psalmist's reference to the "just man," this psalm was used in the Common of Confessors before the Vatican II revision of the missal.

The image of a "tree" predominates today, with the gospel telling us that a good tree produces good fruit; with Sirach saying that "the fruit proves the tree; and with Psalm 92 relating that the just shall "flourish like the palm tree . . . shall produce fruit."

FOR THE JOURNEY

One constantly appearing theme found in the psalter is that God's love for us is "steadfast," namely, God's love is firm, never changing.

This is the type of love we as Christian singers must mirror. We are to labor week after week and year after year in the vocal vineyard. We show our love through loyal attendance at rehearsals— rain or shine, summer or winter. This attendance is a sign of our love for the art of music and for those we serve through this art.

What a wonderful epitaph on a tombstone would be: "Mary Smith, for many years a member of St. Patrick's parish choir. Steadfast in love and service."

STANZA/STROPHE/VERSE

We all know that hymn texts (and much poetry in general) is divided into sections or subdivisions having a number of lines, with each section having a specific pattern of meter and rhyme. These sections are called stanzas or, less frequently, strophes. Musicians often speak of "strophic structure," namely, the same melody being repeated for each stanza (for example, a hymn).

The word "verse" is, in English, also frequently used as a synonym for stanza.

Verse also designates one of the short divisions or lines into which a chapter of the Bible is divided (our present verse divisions are a product of the 16th century).

PRAYER

All powerful Lord,
source of all goodness and beauty,
grant us a spirit of love and fidelity.
May our musical service
lead your people
to the unending joys of your kingdom
where all will share in the fullness
of your glory.

"It would surely be found, that in many parishes, a sufficient number of persons having voices might be found who, with proper instruction from their organist and regular preliminary practice, might relieve the parochial service from the horrid infliction of the charity children's present mode of singing." *Musical Times* (London), June 1844.

Deuteronomy 26:4-10   Psalm 91:1-2, 10-11, 12-13, 14-15
Romans 10:8-13   Luke 4:1-13

R. *Be with me, Lord, when I am in trouble.*

You who live in the shelter of the Most High,
  who abide in the shadow of the Almighty,
will say to the Lord, My refuge and my fortress;
  my God, in whom I trust.

No evil shall befall you,
  no scourge come near your tent.
For he will command his angels concerning you
  to guard you in all your ways.

On their hands they will bear you up,
  so that you will not dash your foot against a stone.
You will tread on the lion and the adder,
  the young lion and the serpent you will trample under
    foot.

Those who love me, I will deliver;
  I will protect those who know my name.
When they call to me, I will answer them;
  I will be with them in trouble.
  I will rescue them and honor them.

The psalmist gives personal testimony while employing various metaphors to point out the favors received from trusting in God. Verses 1-13 are addressed to the chosen people, whereas verses 14-15 give the Lord's response.

According to Luke, the devil quotes this psalm when tempting Jesus in the desert: "If you are the Son of God, throw yourself down from here, for Scripture has it, 'He will command his angels concerning you . . .'"

FOR THE JOURNEY

As Christians we live "on every word that comes from the mouth of God" (Gospel acclamation). It is God's word which is

30

proclaimed in the liturgy, which inspires and sustains so many of our chants and songs. God's word is, in fact, the basis for our prayer together.

Christian devotion down through the centuries has produced many wonderful and time-honored methods of praying. Yet none can surpass the prayers of the Bible, especially the Book of Psalms. These psalms—traditionally attributed to David—are in a special way the singer's book of prayer. Used by generations of Jewish and Christian believers, they express every dimension of life's joys and sorrows.

LENT

The season of Lent (the word comes from the medieval English *lente*, meaning "springtime") began with the custom of Christians observing a fast prior to the Easter Vigil. This fast was extended and, by the 4th century, lasted forty days (*quadragesima*) in imitation of Christ's fasting in the desert.

In addition to fasting, the people practiced almsgiving, came together for prayer and for hearing the word of God. They joined the catechumens preparing for baptism in what might be called a "spiritual retreat."

With the recent restoration of the catechumenate, Lent again offers us an opportunity to accompany the catechumens as they and the whole assembly prepare for the celebration of baptism during the Easter Vigil.

PRAYER

Lord God,
may the power of your word
inflame our hearts
and enliven our song.
Help us to celebrate these forty days
in a spirit of prayer, service, and love.

"There are three things, my brethren, which cause faith to stand firm. They are prayer, fasting, and mercy ... These three are one, and they give life to each other." Peter Chrysologus (c.400-450).

Genesis 15:5-12, 17-18   Psalm 27:1, 7-8, 8-9, 13-14
Philippians 3:17-4:1 or 3:20-4:1   Luke 9:28-36

R. *The Lord is my light and my salvation.*

The Lord is my light and my salvation;
    whom should I fear?
The Lord is the stronghold of my life;
    of whom should I be afraid?

Hear, O Lord, when I cry aloud.
    be gracious to me and answer me!
"Come," my heart says, "seek his face!"
    Your face, Lord, do I seek.

Do not hide your face from me.
Do not turn your servant away in anger,
    you who have been my help,
Do not cast me off.

I believe that I shall see the goodness of the Lord
    in the land of the living.
Wait for the Lord;
    be strong, and let your heart take courage;
    wait for the Lord.

Psalm 27 probably brings together what were originally two distinct psalms. Verses 1-6 are a hymn of confidence; verses 7-14 have been called a "prayer of need" wherein the psalmist confidently requests divine protection.

Today's gospel presents the transfiguration scene; the psalm with its "Your face, Lord, I seek" reflects not only the desire of Peter, John, and James, but that of the whole church.

FOR THE JOURNEY

One of the earliest ways of visually depicting the church is that of the *orans* as found in the art of the catacombs—the church is pictured as a woman standing upright, with hands raised toward heaven.

For centuries standing was the

32

normal position for prayer: recalling the resurrection of Christ, it was the bodily position for offering praise and thanksgiving (except during Lent when kneeling as a sign of penance was enjoined upon the community).

It is normal for choir members to stand while singing during the liturgy. We do so in order to facilitate tone production. And yet as we stand, we do well to recall that we sing because we have been baptized into new life by Christ. No matter what we are singing or when we are singing, we are always resurrection singers.

CAECILIAN MOVEMENT

One of the most influential music reform movements in the Roman Catholic Church is known as "Caecilianism" or the "Caecilian Movement."

Beginning in Bavaria in the mid-nineteenth century, the movement had as its goal to replace the often gaudy, theatrical, and pompous liturgical music of the time through the restoration of Gregorian Chant and classical polyphony. The compositions produced, however, were lifeless imitations of the past, a music divorced from the musical evolution underway at the time.

In the United States the center of Caecilianism was the Catholic Normal School of the Holy Family, which began in 1871 as an adjunct to St. Francis Seminary in Milwaukee. The school's most famous professor (and a prolific composer as well) was John B. Singenberger (1848-1924).

PRAYER

Lord God,
hear our prayers
as we call upon you
with faith and trust.
Strengthen and encourage us
as we sing praise
to the glory of your name.

"Because we are risen with Christ and must seek the things above, on the day of the resurrection we remain standing as a sign that we recall the grace bestowed on us." Basil the Great (c. 330-379).

33

Exodus 3:1-8, 13-15   Psalm 103:1-2, 3-4, 6-7, 8, 11
1 Corinthians 10:1-6, 10-12   Luke 13:1-9

R. *The Lord is kind and merciful.*

Bless the Lord, O my soul,
    and all that is within me,
    bless his holy name.
Bless the Lord, O my soul,
    and do not forget all his benefits.

Who forgives all your iniquity,
    who heals all your diseases,
who redeems your life from the Pit,
    who crowns you with steadfast love and mercy.

The Lord works vindication
    and justice for all who are oppressed.
He made known his ways to Moses,
    his acts to the people of Israel.

The Lord is merciful and gracious
    slow to anger and abounding in steadfast love.
For as the heavens are high above the earth
    so great is his steadfast love toward those who
        fear him.

This hymn of praise and thanksgiving was also used on the 7th Sunday of the Year in Cycle C.

Exodus 3 relates how Moses encountered God in the midst of the burning bush: God has truly acted on behalf of the people. Just as God "made known his ways to Moses," so God will be known by us when we are in need.

FOR THE JOURNEY

The whole Bible is permeated with a sense of the past, with reverence for what God accomplished for "our fathers." This link with our past history is no less evident in our celebration of the Mass and sacraments.

For example, the two principal components of the Mass (i.e., the liturgy of the word and the liturgy of the eucharist) have been celebrated by God's "faithful ones" down through the centuries: in private homes by the early Christians, in remote towns and hamlets, in medieval cathedrals and monasteries, in Nazi and Soviet prison camps, etc. Our ritual activity links us to all those steadfast men and women who have steadfastly preceded us in the faith, who have done what we now do.

By the same token, when we share in the song of the church, we also join the singing of past generations. Styles and melodies may change; nonetheless, it is the same song of faith passed down to us—a song we, in turn, are to hand on to others.

NAVE

A church building has many sections, its principal part being that area called the nave and used by the people. In older buildings, pillars usually separate the nave from the side aisles.

The word "nave" comes from the Latin *navis* (meaning "ship") since early on in Christianity the church building, namely, the house where God's people gather, was viewed as a ship heading on toward its eternal goal.

"When you, as commander of a great ship, call an assembly of the church, appoint the assemblies to be made with all possible skill, charging the deacons as mariners to prepare places for the brethren as for passage . . . let the building be long, with its head to the east . . . and so it will be like a ship." *Apostolic Constitutions* (c.375)

PRAYER

Almighty God,
you have always been present
among your people
to sustain their faith and love.
Help us to offer you
fitting service and praise
as we sing glory to your name.

"The call to 'do penance' is based not on the fact that penance will keep us in trim, but on the fact that 'the Kingdom of Heaven is at hand'." Thomas Merton, *Seasons of Celebration*, 1950.

Joshua 5:9, 10-12   Psalm 34:1-2, 3-4, 5-6
2 Corinthians 5:17-21   Luke 15:1-3, 11-32

R. *Taste and see the goodness of the Lord.*

I will bless the Lord at all times;
    his praise shall continually be in my mouth.
My soul makes its boast in the Lord;
    let the humble hear and be glad.

O magnify the Lord with me,
    and let us exalt his name together.
I sought the Lord, and he answered me,
    and delivered me from all my fears.

Look to him, and be radiant;
    so your faces shall never be ashamed.
This poor soul cried, and was heard by the Lord,
    and was saved from every trouble.

The psalmist not only praises God who has offered protection to the just, but also exhorts others to share in this praise.

Today's gospel speaks of the "banquet" prepared at the return of the prodigal son, whereas the Old Testament selection relates that the people, upon entering the Promised Land, partook of its food. It is in this context that the church can sing Psalm 34 with its antiphon "Taste and see the goodness of the Lord." Thus the psalm becomes, as it were, a eucharistic psalm. We experience the saving presence of God.

FOR THE JOURNEY

The psalmist in today's psalm calls upon others to join in giving thankful praise to God. As is customary for this Jewish poet, all are invited to share in the psalmist's own song of praise and thanksgiving to the Almighty One.

Our ministry is also one of sharing and communicating. Through song we—not unlike the homilist—also communicate

God's message of hope and love. Through music we are reaching out to others so that they may also hear God's message and be touched by it.

PLAINSONG

A term frequently used by church musicians is "plainsong." This word comes from the Latin "cantus planus" and is often used to designate Gregorian Chant.

The term "cantus planus"—which is first documented as early as the 9th century—originally distinguished a "low chant" (*planus*=plane, lying flat) from a *cantus acutus* (a "high chant"). But by the 13th century it referred to the church's "traditional" unison music (now known as Gregorian Chant) as contrasted with the part music then in use.

The word "plainsong" or (more frequently) "chant" is also used for various other types of liturgical music used in western Europe, music using a Latin text. And so we have Ambrosian Chant (Milan), Gallican Chant (Gaul), and Mozarabic or Visigothic Chant (Spain).

The word "chant is also applied to other types of traditional religious music (Hindu chant, Jewish chant, Russian chant).

Common to all these types of music is their emphasis on the melodic character of the music. It is vocal music (as is folksong), and yet it lacks the strict meter and measure we usually find in folksong.

PRAYER

God of power and might,
you call us to give praise
to your name.
Help us to inspire others
to offer joyful song
in your church.

"Teaching people the language of music . . . means forming to community to know its voice. It means leading the community to believe that its song is essential. Evoking such an attitude and building a community's confidence in their song is the first responsibility of all liturgical-musical leadership." *The Milwaukee Symposia for Church Composers: A Ten-Year Report* no. 20 (1992).

Isaiah 43:16-21   Psalm 126:1-2, 2-3, 4-5, 6
Philippians 3:8-14   John 8:1-11

R. *The Lord has done great things for us;*
  we are filled with joy.

When the Lord restored the fortunes of Zion,
  we were like those who dream.
Then our mouth was filled with laughter,
  and our tongue with shouts of joy.

Then it was said among the nations,
  "The Lord has done great things for them."
The Lord has done great things for us,
  and we rejoiced.

Restore our fortunes, O Lord,
like the watercourses in the Hegeb.
May those who sow in tears
  reap with shouts of joy.

Those who go out weeping,
  bearing the seed for sowing,
shall come home with shouts of joy,
  carrying their sheaves.

Psalm 126 is also used on the Second Sunday of Advent in the C Cycle.

It is in light of today's gospel (Christ forgiving the adulterous woman) that the first reading can be understood. "See, I am doing something new" (Is 43:19). "The Lord has done great things for us" and continues to do so. This is the reason for our hope and our joy.

FOR THE JOURNEY

The early church considered the Sunday gathering for word and eucharist to be foundational for the church's very existence (the Lord's people gathering on the Lord's day to celebrate the Lord's supper). In fact, for many centuries failure to gather with the church was considered as scattering the church and weakening its unity, a unity expressed in many ways, including song.

For numerous reasons this foundational role of the people at Sunday Mass came to be weakened, and it was only restored by the liturgical reforms initiated by Vatican II. The primary celebrant of the liturgy is once again seen to be the body of the faithful who have come together to offer praise to God.

So it is that the singing voices of all the people are the foundation of the liturgy's musical expression. All our efforts as choir members and singers are directed to encouraging, sustaining, and enhancing the common song of all. It is this common song that we serve. Without this common song, we lose the meaning of our ministry.

NEUMES

We all know what notes are, but what are "neumes"?

A neume (from the Greek "*neuma*" meaning a nod or a sign) is simply the term for a note (or cluster of notes) in Gregorian Chant and in similar systems of music (e.g., Byzantine chant).

In Gregorian Chant some neumes signify single notes; others cluster of two, three, or more notes.

In the earliest manuscripts of Gregorian Chant the neumes give only the general contours of the melodic line—they were merely an aid to the singer's memory. Only in the 11th century did the use of a staff (thus indicating intervals) become popular. Chant notation today continues to use a four line staff.

PRAYER

All powerful and loving God,
you call us to form one people,
one body united in Christ.
Help us to be faithful servants
of those who gather
to give praise to your name.

"If it is desired that the liturgical assembly be initiated, educated, and guided in its singing, a choir is indispensable." Letter by Cardinal Lercaro (25 January 1966).

Isaiah 50:4-7   Psalm 22:7-8, 16-17, 18-19, 22-23
Philippians 2:6-11   Luke 22:14-23:56 or 23:1-49

R. My God, my God, why have you abandoned me?

All who see me mock at me;
    they make mouths at me, they shake their heads;
"Commit your cause to the Lord, let him deliver—
    let him rescue the one in whom he delights.

For dogs are all around me;
    a company of evildoers encircles me.
My hands and feet have shriveled;
    I can count all my bones.

They divide my clothes among themselves,
    and for my clothing they cast lots.
But you, O Lord, do not be far away!
    O my help, come quickly to my aid!

I will tell of your name to my brothers and sisters;
    in the midst of the congregation I will praise you.
You who fear the Lord, praise him!
    All you offspring of Jacob, glorify him.

Psalm 22, a messianic psalm which Christianity has traditionally applied to Christ, appears to have originally been three separate psalms: verses 2-22 - a song of despair; verses 23-27 - a call to praise; verses 28-32 - a declaration that all people will worship God.

Many verses from this psalm can be found in the Passion accounts read during Holy Week: for example, the second verse "My God, my God ..." (used as the antiphon) is placed upon the lips of Jesus on the cross.

FOR THE JOURNEY

Holy Week concludes with the Easter Triduum, which begins on Holy Thursday with the Mass of the Lord's Supper and continues on till Easter Sunday. Initiated in the city of Jerusalem where the people relived each event of the paschal mystery, these days in fact relive but a single event, namely, the total mystery of Christ's redemptive love for us, even though each day highlights a particular aspect of this mystery.

The Easter Triduum has been called the climax of the liturgical year; it is the Christian "high holy days." During these days we in a special way join Christ in his victory over death. Our song, no matter what the words, is a song of hope: the struggle of Christ is our struggle; his victory is our victory.

THE PASSION ACCOUNTS

Beginning in the 12th century the custom arose of dramatizing, as it were, the Passion accounts read during Holy Week; and yet the papal liturgy at Rome long resisted this practice.

The part of Christ (*vox Christi*) was sung in the lowest register and in a slow and solemn fashion. That of the narrator, who was called the *evangelista* or *chronista*, was in a middle register and given in a normal speed and character. That of the crowd (the *turba Judaeorum*) was in a high range and was delivered with speed and agitation.

In the most ancient book the parts were indicated by the letters t (*tarde* = slowly), c (*celeriter* = quickly) and a (*alta voce*); in more recent books the signs + (Christ), C (chronista), and S (synagogue) were used.

Today, however, the passion is usually read by three ministers, often with musical interventions by the assembly.

PRAYER

Almighty and everlasting God,
as we prepare for the celebration of the Lord's
death and resurrection,
help us so that our song
may ever proclaim the wonders
your Son has gained for us.

"The praise of the one you sing to is the singers themselves. Do you want to offer praise to God? Be yourselves what you sing." Augustine, *Homily on Psalm 149*.

Acts 10:34, 37-43   Psalm 118:1-2, 16-17, 22-23
Colossians 3:1-4 or Corinthians 5:6-8   John 20:1-9

> R. *This is the day the Lord has made;*
>   *let us rejoice and be glad.*
>
> O give thanks to the Lord, for he is good;
>   his steadfast love endures forever!
> Let Israel say,
>   "His steadfast love endures forever."
>
> "The right hand of the Lord is exalted;
>   the right hand of the Lord does valiantly."
> I shall not die, but I shall live,
>   and recount the deeds of the Lord.
>
> The stone that the builders rejected
>   has become the chief cornerstone.
> This is the Lord's doing;
>   it is marvelous in our eyes.

In Psalm 118 the psalmist speaks in the name of the whole nation as he gives thanks to the Lord. It has been suggested that this psalm was originally composed for liturgical purposes.

This psalm is the traditional Easter psalm in the Catholic Church. We, together with Christ, have been rescued from death; we will indeed recount the deeds of the Lord. Verse 24 "This is the day . . ." is used as the antiphon.

FOR THE JOURNEY

Each year the Christian calendar brings us certain major feasts. For example, we are called to observe Easter, the day when Christ rose unto new life. Celebrated year after year, Easter is an annual landmark as we progress onward in our Christian journey.

But there is a danger here. Easter is the major feast of the church, a feast that demands our joyous cries of Alleluia. And we certainly want to use all the forces in our artistic repertory to express the beauty and wonder of this day. But if we are to do this in all truth, we must first allow the risen Christ to take hold of us and transform us with new life. The power of the resurrected Lord must be unleashed in our hearts and in our lives. Only then can we truly sing Alleluia. Only then can our Easter song be authentic.

ALLELUIA

From the Hebrew *hallelu-jah* ("praise the Lord"), the word "Alleluia" is an expression of joy and praise.

In the Hebrew Bible the word occurs only in conjunction with the psalms: either before the psalm, after the psalm, or both.

At an early date the Alleluia was introduced into the Roman liturgy, and by the time of Pope Gregory the Great (590-604) its use was extended throughout the entire year, except during Lent.

An early medieval practice (called the "*jubilus*") was to have an extended melismatic vocalization sung on the final syllable ("a") of the Alleluia.

According to one author, the Alleluia was sung over and over again in the Coptic Church (Ethiopia)—up to a quarter of an hour.

The Alleluia, always sung by the whole assembly, remains a sign of joy, especially the joy of the resurrection. We rejoice in the victory of the Lamb over sin and death.

PRAYER

All powerful God,
by the Easter mystery
you have raised us
to new life in Christ.
Help us so that our voices
may sing of Christ's power and
presence among us.

"It is called jubulus because neither by words, nor syllables, nor letters, nor voice, can it be expressed or comprehended how much man ought to praise God." Pseudo-Jerome (7th century?).

43

Acts 5:12-16   Psalm 118:2-4, 13-15, 22-24
Revelation 1:9-11, 12-13, 17-19   John 20:19-31

R. *Give thanks to the Lord for he is good,*
   his love is everlasting.

Let Israel say,
   "His steadfast love endures forever."
Let the house of Aaron say,
   "His steadfast love endures forever."
Let those who fear the Lord say,
   "His steadfast love endures forever."

I was pushed hard, so that I was falling,
   but the Lord helped me.
The Lord is my strength and my might;
   he has become my salvation.
There are glad songs of victory
   in the tents of the righteous.

The stone that the builders rejected
   has become the chief cornerstone.
This is the Lord's doing;
   it is marvelous in our eyes.
This is the day that the Lord has made;
   let us rejoice and be glad in it.

As on last Sunday, today's psalm is again Psalm 118.

The Acts of the Apostles today relate how the sick and disturbed were brought to the apostles who, as a sign of their divine mission, cured them. And yet this was the result of the Lord at work (see Ps 118:13-15); for this reason the community is called upon to "give thanks to the Lord."

FOR THE JOURNEY

Life on this planet would be a swirl of confusion if we lacked signs that guide us in our daily lives: signs that tell us to "go" and to "stop," signs that tell us by which door to depart, signs warning us that a bottle contains a harmful liquid.

44

Signs are no less important for our lives as Christians: the tolling of the church bell, the use of flowers to decorate the sanctuary and other areas in the church, the first singing of the Alleluia during the Easter Vigil, celibacy as a freely chosen way of living out the Gospel, etc.

We might not always be aware of it, but the choir itself is a sign.

The presence of the choir, whose members witness dedication, self-sacrifice, and artistic achievement, is itself a sign to the assembly that "something important is happening here." What we are about has to do with something special. It concerns the Lord, the Lord's day, the Lord's people, and the Lord's meal.

MOTET

Each year most choirs learn several new "motets." From the French *mot* ("word"), a motet is a choral composition with a religious (usually Latin) text and originally unaccompanied.

This type of composition arose in the 13th century and throughout history has known many and varied forms: e.g., motets for soloist, motets with orchestral accompaniment, motets with vernacular texts.

Today the term "motet" is often applied to a wide variety of choral compositions (both accompanied and unaccompanied) destined for church use.

PRAYER

Most loving Father,
you call us together
to celebrate Christ's resurrection
in our lives.
May our song of praise
increase the faith of
all who gather
to celebrate your name.

"And so more sweetly pleasing to God than any musical instrument would be the symphony of the people of God, by which in every church of God, with kindred spirit and single disposition, with one mind and unanimity of faith and piety, we raise melody in unison in our psalmody." Eusebius of Caesaria (c.260-c.340).

Acts 5:27-32, 40-41   Psalm 30:1, 3, 4-5, 10-11, 12
Revelation 5:11-14   John 21:1-19 or 21:1-14

R. *I will praise you, Lord, for you have rescued me.*

I will extol you, O Lord, for you have drawn
      me up,
   and did not let my foes rejoice over me.
O Lord, you brought up my soul for Sheol,
   restored me to life from among those gone
      down to the Pit.

Sing praises to the Lord, O you his faithful ones,
   and give thanks to his holy name.
For his anger is but for a moment;
   his favor is for a lifetime.
Weeping may linger for the night,
   but joy comes with the morning.

"Hear, O Lord, and be gracious to me!
   O Lord, be my helper!"
You have turned my mourning into dancing;
   O Lord my God, I will give thanks to you
      forever.

The psalmist thanks God for having been restored to health and for having been delivered from death.

In today's first reading we are told that the apostles departed from the Sanhedrin "full of joy that they had been judged worthy of ill-treatment for the sake" of Jesus' name. Indeed, in the words of today's psalm, God changed their "mourning into dancing." No suffering goes unnoticed by the Lord. In the end there is always rejoicing.

FOR THE JOURNEY

It has often been observed that the liturgical renewal experienced in the Roman Catholic Church (and in other churches) would never have been success- ful without the faithful dedication and commitment of thousands of volunteers.

So many people have joyfully given of themselves and their talents . . . readers, planners, musicians—to mention just a few.

But no group has contributed more of its time and talent than our choir members with weekly rehearsals throughout the year, with the many personal sacrifices of being present Sunday after Sunday at a specific liturgy.

As a choir member you love music; as serving the Christian assembly you love your brothers and sisters in Christ. And to you this assembly simply says "Thank you. Our celebrations, our prayer, are indeed richer because of you."

ANTHEM

An anthem (from the old English *antefn*, a word derived from the Greek "antiphona") is a choral composition with English words (from Scripture, religious poetry) and often accompanied by organ. In a sense, an anthem is the English equivalent of the Latin motet. The anthem has its origins in the Anglican Church when, as a result of the English Reformation, there was a need for musical settings of English texts.

Compared to the traditional motet, the text of an anthem is generally more syllabic with shorter phrases. One of our century's most noted composer of anthems was the Englishman Ralph Vaughn Williams (1872-1958).

PRAYER

Almighty God,
source of all goodness and love,
we thank you
for all you have done for us.
Help us to faithfully serve
our brothers and sisters
through the beauty of song.

"Your presence is needed at all levels; besides your service as a group, the support that each of you individually can give to your own church and parish takes away nothing from your function, your tastes, your good will. Your function as choirs continues to be invaluable, indeed irreplaceable . . . Carry out your mission with joy, with love, with reverence, and with dedication." Paul VI (6 April 1970).

Acts 13:14, 43-52   Psalm 100:1-2, 3, 5
Revelation 7:9, 14-17   John 10:27-30

> R. *We are his people: the sheep of his flock.*
>
> Make a joyful noise to the Lord, all the earth.
>   Worship the Lord with gladness;
>   come into his presence with singing.
>
> Know that the Lord is God.
>   It is he that made us, and we are his;
>   we are his people and the sheep of his pasture.
>
> For the Lord is good;
>   his steadfast love endures forever,
>   and his faithfulness to all generations.

This very short psalm, which may have been sung at the people's solemn entry into the temple, summons the people to give praise.

In today's gospel we hear Jesus telling us that "my sheep hear my voice . . ." The Book of Revelation refers to the Lamb who will shepherd the people. We, in turn, acknowledge that we are God's people, the "sheep of his pasture."

FOR THE JOURNEY

Theologians like to remind us that when we come together for worship on Sunday, we do not do so of our own initiative. We assemble because God has called us together. God's initiative comes first. We, for our part, are responding to this summons.

Because our response to God is affirmative, there is church, namely the body of Christ assembled together; and there can be no church without its members coming together for common prayer.

In similar manner, those of us who are singers are also asked to respond to God's initiative. We are called to lend our talents, our voices, in a special way to this assembly convoked by Almighty God.

A canticle (from the Latin "*canticulum*" meaning "little song") is a song-like text found in the Scriptures and yet taken from a Book other than the Book of Psalms.

There are two categories of canticles.

The major or greater canticles (*cantica maiora*) are taken from the New Testament, e.g., the *Magnificat* (Lk 1:46-55), the *Nunc dimittis* (Lk 2L29-32), and the *Benedictus* (Lk 1:68-79). These canticles traditionally appear in the liturgy of the hours.

The minor or lesser canticles are from the Old Testament and include, among others, the "*Cantemus Domino*" (from Ex 15) and the Song of David (1 Chr 29:10-18).

Canticles are an important part of our musical heritage.

PRAYER

Most loving Father,
you gather us together
as your family,
as your people.
Make us able and willing
to use our gifts
in offering praise to your name.

"Several years ago, on a Sunday morning, I entered the cathedral of Cologne, during a low Mass, and took a seat in the body of the church. The vast edifice was filled with a devout congregation, representing every station in life. I observed the officer and the private soldier, the well-dressed gentleman and the plainly clad laborer, ladies and domestics, young and old, priests and laymen, mingled together and singing in the vernacular, the popular sacred hymns of father-land. They seemed so absorbed in their devotional chant, as to be utterly oblivious of every thing around them. I said to myself: What a noble profession of faith this is!" James Cardinal Gibbons, Archbishop of Baltimore, *The Ambassador of Christ* (1896).

Fifth Sunday of Easter — May 14, 1995

Acts 14:21-27 Psalm 145:8-9, 10-11, 12-13
Revelation 21:1-5 John 13:31-33, 34-35

R. *I will praise your name for ever, my king and my God.*

The Lord is gracious and merciful,
   slow to anger and abounding in steadfast love.
The Lord is good to all,
   and his compassion is over all that he has made.

All your works shall give thanks to you, O Lord,
   and all your faithful shall bless you.
They shall speak of the glory of your kingdom,
   and tell of your power.

They shall make known to all people your mighty deeds,
   and the glorious splendor of your kingdom.
Your kingdom is an everlasting kingdom,
   and your dominion endures throughout all generations.

It is God the King, the almighty and provident God, whom the psalmist praises in this psalm, many of whose phrases we can find elsewhere in the Bible.

In today's first reading Paul and Barnabas encourage their disciples to persevere: "We must undergo many trials if we are to enter the reign of God." God's kingdom, in the words of the psalmist, "is a kingdom for all ages . . ." Its character is timeless.

FOR THE JOURNEY

Today's gospel is about being good servants, being loving servants.

Our mission in the liturgy is to serve the assembly. Our task is to assist the members of the

50

assembly in their prayer. We do so primarily by supporting and enhancing the voice of the people upraised in sung prayer. We also do so by creating a musical environment for prayer.

And yet we must be modest servants. We can never cause prayer to happen. Music is not to manipulate but to free. We can only create conditions within which people, with God's help, can respond to the promptings of the Spirit dwelling in their hearts.

CANTATA

Some choirs, especially during Advent or Lent, gives special concerts during which they perform what are known as cantatas. A cantata is a choral work, with instrumental accompaniment, usually containing arias, duets, choruses, and based upon a continuous narrative.

The cantata first appeared in the early 17th century and reached its artistic peack with the compositions of J.S. Bach (1685-1750) who wrote close to 300 of these compositions.

Many of the early cantatas were secular in nature, as some are today.

PRAYER

Lord God,
fill us with the power of Christ
who came to live in this world
as the servant of all.
Help us to be faithful servants
of your church's prayerful song.

"... do not cut yourselves off from the requirements of the rites or forget the needs of the congregation. Do not shut yourselves up, contrary to God's will, in narcissistic complacency over your singing virtuosity and artistic abilities. Rather, know well how to give real guidance to the assembly ... by inspiring the people to sing, by raising the level of their taste, by arousing their desire to take part." Paul VI (6 April 1970).

Acts 15:1-2, 22-29   Psalm 67:1-2, 4, 5, 7
Revelation 21:10-14, 22-23   John 14:23-29

R. *O God, let all the nations praise you!*

My God be gracious to us and bless us
  and make his face to shine upon us,
that your way may be known upon earth,
  your saving power among all nations.

Let the nations be glad and sing for joy,
  for you judge the peoples with equity
  and guide the nations upon the earth.

Let the peoples praise you, O God,
  let all the peoples praise you.
May God continue to bless us;
  let all the ends of the earth revere him.

Psalm 67, believed by some to have been composed for a harvest festival, calls on all nations to praise the Lord.

Today's reading from the Acts of the Apostles recounts that the church was aware of its mission to be a universal church, a church that would not place undue burdens on Gentile converts. Both Jew and Gentile—all the nations—are called to praise God.

FOR THE JOURNEY

One of the New Testament expressions for the eucharist is the "breaking of the bread." The early Christian community recognized the Lord in the breaking of the bread. And among the fruits of sharing in this breaking are unity and peace.

Unfortunately, many divisions afflict the church today. At times we even find a mean-spiritedness masquerading under the guise of orthodoxy. In the wake of Vatican II divisions continue.

At times these even invade groups of ministers: petty jealousies, rivalries, misunderstandings—all are obstacles to love and unity.

Just as we meet the Lord in the breaking of the bread, we also meet the Lord when we break down barriers, and especially those found among our choir membership. It is only then that we can sing with one mind and one heart.

A jewel within the church's glorious tradition of sung prayer is the *Te Deum*, which is a hymn of praise and thanksgiving. It was once sung at the conclusion of matins in the Divine Office on certain feasts.

This extended doxology begins with a series of exclamations praising God the Father.

> We praise you, O God;
> > we acclaim you, Lord and Master.
> Everlasting Father,
> > all the world bows down before you. Etc.

Then comes a Christological section.

> O Christ, the King of glory!
> You alone are the Father's eternal Son . . .

The hymn concludes with a series of petitions.

> We therefore implore You to grant Your servants grace
> > and aid . . .
> Admit them to the ranks of Your saints . . .

Since the Middle Ages this hymn (some people call it a canticle) has been attributed to various authors, including St. Ambrose and St. Augustine. The original author is unknown, but there is some evidence it might have been Niceta of Remesiana (now Nish, Serbia) who died after 414.

Many noted composers (e.g., Handel, Berlioz, Bruckner, Dvorak, Verdi) have set this magnificent text to music.

PRAYER

God of mercy and love,
may our sharing in the eucharist
help us overcome
whatever hinders the unity
of our common song.

"Who can consider as an enemy one with whom he has sung God's praises with one voice? Hence singing the psalms imparts the highest good, love, for it uses communal singing, so to speak, as a bond of unity, and it harmoniously draws people to the symphony of one choir." Basil the Great (c.330-379).

Acts 7:55-60   Psalm 97:1-2, 6-7, 9
Revelation 22:12-14, 16-17, 20   John 17:20-26

R. *The Lord is king, the most high over all the earth.*

The Lord is king! Let the earth rejoice;
    let the many coastlands be glad!
Righteousness and justice are the foundation of
    his throne.

The heavens proclaim his righteousness;
    and all the people behold the glory.
All gods bow down before him.

For you, O Lord, are most high over all the earth;
    you are exalted far above all gods.

Psalm 97, another "kingship psalm, confidently proclaims the coming of the Lord as king and judge.

The Acts of the Apostles relates how Stephen, looking up, saw God's glory and the risen Christ standing at "God's right hand." As the psalmist tells us, God is indeed the king; God is "the most high over all the earth." The Lord reigns supreme.

FOR THE JOURNEY

For centuries church authorities forbade the use of instrumental music within the liturgy. The concern was twofold. In ancient Greece and Rome instrumental music was closely associated with the pagan religion.

But of equal concern was another factor. Unity—the unity for which Jesus prays in today's gospel—was especially to be manifested at each liturgical assembly—and this unity was expressed in common song. When many voices sing, there is—as it were—one voice. And to introduce instrumental music into the liturgy would be to divide the oneness of song coming from the one body.

Today our task as a choir is to further this unity of the assembly. Whether we are are supporting the song of the assembly or adding a choir's particular selection to a celebration, there is to be but one melody, a single choir, whereby earth imitates heaven.

54

There is to be but one voice, a voice mirroring our unity of faith in the one Jesus Christ who is our Lord and King.

GLORY TO GOD

The Glory to God (in Latin known as the *Gloria in excelsis*) is a very ancient Christian hymn. It is one of the few surviving remnants of songs written for the early church's liturgy. Their texts resemble those of the Bible, especially the psalms, and yet they were composed by private individuals (and thus called *"psalmi idiotici"*) as opposed to the inspired biblical texts.

To some extent the *Gloria* is simply an extension of a series of acclamations. It begins with the song of the angels at the first Christmas:

Glory to God in the highest . . .

The hymn continues by praising God:

Lord God, heavenly King . . .

Christ is then invoked:

Lord Jesus Christ, only Son of the Father . . .

This hymn was first used during morning prayer in the eastern church. By the year 500 it was sung on Christmas in Rome. Soon its use spread to all bishops on Sundays and feasts of the martyrs, and then to all priests.

Today the *Gloria* is used on Sundays outside Advent and Lent as well as on solemnities and feasts. Ideally, the Glory to God, being a hymn, is sung—by the people, the people with the choir, or (at times) by the choir alone.

PRAYER

Lord God,
you have raised your Son from the dead
and clothed us with new life.
Help us sing your praises
with confidence, with trust,
and with love.

"All musical instruments accepted for divine worship must be played in such a way as to meet the requirements of a liturgical service and to contribute to the beauty of worship and the building up of the faithful." *Instruction on Music in the Liturgy* (5 March 1967).

Acts 2:1-11   Psalm 104:1, 24, 29-30, 31, 34
1 Corinthians 12:3-7, 12-13   John 20:19-23

R. *Lord, send out your Spirit,*
   and renew the face of the earth.

Bless the Lord, O my soul.
   O Lord my God, you are very great.
O Lord, how manifold are your works!
   The earth is full of your creatures.

When you take away their breath, they die
   and return to their dust.
When you send forth your spirit, they are created;
   and you renew the face of the ground.

May the glory of the Lord endure forever;
   may the Lord rejoice in his works.
May my meditation be pleasing to him,
   for I rejoice in the Lord.

Here the psalmist, exhibiting gratitude to God, praises God's wisdom and extols certain wonderful features of creation. The world depends on God, on the divine breath, as it were.

All the readings today focus on the Holy Spirit who will "renew the face of the earth." As Christians we have indeed been renewed and transformed through the Spirit-filled waters of baptism. We have been anointed with the power of the life-giving Spirit. We are also called to "renew the face of the earth." God's Spirit works through us; God's work is our work.

FOR THE JOURNEY

Jesus, if we are to believe the evangelists, did a lot of talking during his life upon earth. But on the other hand, Jesus was also a good listener, a person who knew how to be receptive to the spoken and unspoken needs of other people.

As choral singers we also need to be listeners: not only are we to listen to (and heed) the coaching of our director; we also need to listen to our own voices and to the voices of the other singers.

Furthermore, we are to listen to (and support) the voices of the assembly.

But above all, we need be attentive to the voice of the Holy Spirit whose song comes to us in so many ways each day.

SEQUENCE

Today, Pentecost Sunday, is among the few days during the liturgical year when there is a sequence. A sequence (from the Latin *sequi* meaning "to follow") was originally a text added to the vocalization over the final vowel of the Alleluia to facilitate memorization of the melody by the singers.

Although less widespread in Rome and Italy, such compositions provided very popular in France and Germany, where almost every Mass had its own sequence.

Simple melodies—often one note per syllable—invited sung participation by the whole assembly. The popular character of these texts resulted in the sequence giving rise to a number of German hymn texts; for example, the German *"Komm, Heiliger Geist"* ("Come, Holy Ghost") derives from the Pentecost sequence.

In the liturgical reform following the Council of Trent the number of these lyrical compositions was dramatically reduced:

Easter: *Victimae paschali laudes* (Wipo)
Pentecost: *Veni sancte spiritus* (Stephen Langton)
Corpus Christi: *Lauda Sion* (Thomas Aquinas)
Requiem: *Dies Irae* (Thomas of Celano)

Today sequences (both a prose and a poetic version appear in the missal) are optional except on Easter and Pentecost. And they occur before the Alleluia.

PRAYER

All-powerful and loving God,
we praise you and bless you.
May the fire of your Spirit
warm our hearts
so that we may sing your praise
with love and devotion.

"The church needs the arts especially for its liturgy which—all in all—is meant to be a work of art inspired by faith, drawing upon all the creative forces of architecture, sculpture and painting, music and poetry." John Paul II (12 September 1983).

Proverbs 8:22-31   Psalm 8:3-4, 5-6, 7-8
Romans 5:1-5   John 16:12-15

R. *O Lord, our God,*
   how wonderful your name in all the earth!

When I look at your heavens,
   the work of your fingers,
   the moon and the stars that
   you have established;
what are human beings that you
   are mindful of them,
   mortals that you care for them?

Yet you have made them a little lower than God,
   and crowned them with glory and honor.
You have given them dominion
   over the works of your hands;
   you have put all things under their feet.

All sheep and oxen,
   and also the beasts of the field,
the birds of the air, and the fish of the sea,
   whatever passes along the paths of the seas.

Psalm 8 begins by praising the majesty of God and continues by extolling the dignity of the human person, who is considered as partaking in ruling over creation.

This Sunday's reading from the Book of Proverbs speaks of God's Wisdom through whom all creation came into existence. The heavens and the earth are indeed the "work" of God's fingers.

FOR THE JOURNEY

Our purpose as choir members is to sing, to make song, to turn notes on a page into a beautiful and prayerful musical rendition. In a way, the choir is very "product" oriented. The rubrics tell us what to do and where to do it.

But what happens after we finish singing a particular piece

in the liturgy? Does this "post-product" time become an occasion for fixing one's hair, for conveying musical directions, or for exchanging pleasantries?

Or do we join the other members of the assembly in giving our total attention to and in participating in the liturgical action in progress?

CLEF

One of the basic building blocks of music is the "clef." By clef (from the Latin "*clavis*" meaning "key) we mean a sign placed at the beginning of a staff to indicate a specific pitch.

As singers there are two clefs we may meet: The G-clef and the F-clef.

The G-clef or treble clef indicates that the note g is on the 2nd line of the staff.

The F-clef or bass clef tells us that the note f is written on the 4th line of the staff.

Sopranos and altos use the G-clef; basses sing from the F-clef; and tenors use the F-clef or—if there is a separate clef for each part—the G-clef.

G-clef: F-clef:

PRAYER

We praise your name, O God,
Father, Son, and Holy Spirit.
Open our hearts
so that our voices
may truly sing
praise to you,
one God in three persons.

"Psalms and hymns sound between the two of them [i.e., the pious husband and wife] and they challenge each other to see who better sings to the Lord. Seeing and hearing this, Christ rejoices." Tertullian (c.170-c.225).

Genesis 14:18-20   Psalm 110:1, 2, 3, 4
1 Corinthians 11:23-26   Luke 9:11-17

R. *You are a priest for ever,*
  in the line of Melchizedek.

The Lord says to my lord,
  "Sit at my right hand
until I make your enemies your footstool."

The Lord sends out from Zion
  your mighty scepter,
  Rule in the midst of your foes.

From the womb of the morning,
    like dew, your youth will come to you.

The Lord has sworn and will not change his
    mind,
  "You are a priest forever according to the
    order of Melchizedek."

One of the most poetic compositions in the psalter (and also one of the most difficult to interpret), Psalm 110 is a messianic hymn extolling the Messiah as king, priest, and victor.

The Messiah, according to the psalmist, will be a "priest forever according to the order of Melchizedek." The Book of Genesis tells us that Melchizedek, King of Salem, said a prayer of blessing over the bread and wine—thus prefiguring Christ and his gift to us of the eucharist.

The priesthood of Melchizedek prefigures our participation in Christ's priesthood; we are all priests through baptism; whereas some of us share in Christ's priesthood by reason of ordination.

So important was the person of Melchizedek in the early church that he is mentioned in the Roman Canon which speaks of the "bread and wine offered by your priest Melchisedech."

FOR THE JOURNEY

The second reading for today's feast, which developed in the 13th century to solemnly honor the Blessed Sacrament, is from St. Paul who gives us one of the classic accounts of how the Lord instituted the eucharist.

The ongoing miracle of the eucharist is that, after praise and glory are given to God, the Holy Spirit comes to change bread and wine into the Lord's body and blood—and we, by receiving these gifts, are also changed into the Body of Christ, and this also through the work of the Spirit.

But for this to happen, we have to be open to the Spirit in our lives; we have to make room for the Spirit to transform our individual voices, with all their imperfections, into the one, perfect voice of Christ's Body, the church.

_____ GUIDO OF AREZZO _____

Throughout history the Benedictine monks have greatly influenced not only the liturgy of the church but also the chant of the church and even general techniques used for singing. A case in point is the practice whereby singers learn melodies through the use of the syllables "do, re, mi," etc.

The inventor of this method was a Benedictine monk, Guido, who was born toward the end of the 10th century. Even though he was born in Paris, Guido was responsible for a choir school at Arezzo in Italy.

To facilitate the teaching of melodies to the choir boys, Guido associated each note of a hexichord (a scale of 6 notes) with a particular syllable, "ut [now called 'do'], re, mi, fa, sol, la"—each of these syllable began successive lines of the Gregorian hymn "Ut queant laxis," and the initial notes of each line were successively C, D, E, F, G, A.

The use of such syllables, called solemnization, has assisted generations of singers to read music.

PRAYER

Lord, Jesus Christ,
your gift to us
is the sacrament of your body and
blood.
Transform our hearts
so that our lips may truly sing
songs of joyful praise
to the glory of your name.

". . . the liturgy on earth will fuse with that of heaven where . . . it will form one choir . . . to praise with one voice the Father through Jesus Christ." John Paul II (4 December 1988).

Zechariah 12:10-11   Psalm 63:1, 2-3, 4-5, 7-8
Galatians 3:26-29   Luke 9:18-24

R. *My soul is thirsting for you, O Lord my God.*

O God, you are my God, I seek you,
    my soul thirsts for you;
my flesh faints for you,
    as in a dry and weary land where there is no water.

So I have looked upon you in the sanctuary,
    beholding your power and glory.
Because your steadfast love is better than life,
    my lips will praise you.

So I will bless you as long as I live;
    I will lift up my hands and call on your name.
My soul is satisfied as with a rich feast,
    and my mouth praises you with joyful lips.

For you have been my help,
    and in the shadow of your wings I sing for joy.
My soul clings to you;
    your right hand upholds me.

This is the song of a person who longs for God. The psalmist is pictured as being in the desert which is dry and without water.

Today's first reading seems to refer to a future cosmic battle when someone (the Messiah?) will be slain. Perhaps it was for this reason that Psalm 63 ("steadfast love is better than life") was chosen as today's responsorial psalm.

FOR THE JOURNEY

Liturgy, like life, is full of paradoxes. Liturgy speaks of longing for the Lord, and yet we know that Christ is present among us when we gather for prayer. This, for example, is why monks have traditionally faced one another as they pray.

There are other forms of Christ's presence as well: in his

word, in his minister, in the eucharist, in the celebration of the sacraments.

And when we sing together, we acknowledge that we are one in Christ who dwells in our midst. Our song is the song of Christ; our prayer is the prayer of Christ, for we are the Body of Christ.

PSALTER

A book common to Jewish and Christian liturgical practice is the "psalter," the word being a general term referring to a book that contains the psalms. For example:

- the Book of Psalms as found in the Bible itself;
- a book containing metrical versions of the psalms;
- a book containing the psalms as arranged for use in the divine office or the liturgy of the hours.

The psalter has been called the "believer's prayer book." It can also be called the church's liturgical prayer book; much of the church's music is psalmody; and even its hymnody has been greatly influenced by psalm texts.

Tradition ascribes the authorship of the psalms to King David, and yet it appears that the Book of Psalms was formed over many centuries. Many of the psalms also appear to have originated in Jewish liturgical ritual.

PRAYER

God of love,
we rejoice
in the gift of your presence among us.
Open our hearts
so that the songs we sing
may reflect
our unity in Christ.

"A psalm is tranquility of soul and the arbitration of peace; it settles one's tumultuous and seething thoughts. It mollifies the soul's wrath and chastens its recalcitrance. A psalm creates friendships, unites the separated, and reconciles those at enmity." Basil the Great (c.330-379).

1 Kings 19:16, 19-21 · Psalm 16:1-2, 5, 7-8, 9-10, 11
Galatians 5:1, 13-18 · Luke 9:51-62

R. *You are my inheritance, O Lord.*

Protect me, O God, for in you I take refuge.
I say to the Lord, "You are my Lord."
The Lord is my chosen portion and my cup;
 you hold my lot.

I bless the Lord who gives me counsel;
 in the night also my heart instructs me.
I keep the Lord always before me;
 because he is at my right hand, I shall not be moved.

Therefore my heart is glad, and my soul rejoices;
 my body also rests secure.
For you do not give me up to Sheol,
 or let your faithful ones see the Pit.

You show me the path of life.
 In your presence there is fullness of joy;
 in your right hand are pleasures forevermore.

The psalmist proclaims an awareness of God's caring presence.

God will show the psalmist "the path to life." This is the path the disciples of Jesus follow as they respond in today's gospel to the Lord's command, "Come after me." Christ our inheritance show us how to obtain true life. He guides us on our journey to the kingdom. He is indeed the "way, the truth, and the light."

FOR THE JOURNEY

Just as the church as a whole requires various services (that of pastors, prophets, catechists, those working on behalf of the poor, those striving to bring about peace and justice . . .), so too does the church's liturgy (which is to mirror the very reality of the church) need a variety of services and thus people to carry out these services. And so one of the hallmarks of liturgy is a diversity of ministers—presiders, deacons, readers, can-

64

tors, singers, etc. But these ministers do not function in isolation from one another; they either support one another (Paul in today's second reading tells us to "be servants of one another") or weaken one another.

When, for example, a reader proclaims God's word with faith and conviction, he or she facilitates the ministry of the homilist who breaks open this word in the homily.

Or when we, as members of a choral group, focus our attention on the cantor who is delivering the psalm verses, then we are supporting the cantor's ministry. No minister stands apart from other ministers. Ministries depend upon other ministries.

RESPONSORIAL PSALMODY

Responsorial psalmody is the practice, so well-known to most of us, whereby a soloist (or even a choir) sings the verses of a psalm, and the whole assembly responds by singing a short and simple refrain after each verse or section of a verse.

Some believe that Christians inherited this style of singing the psalms from the synagogue.

Psalm 136, for example, concludes each verse with "for his steadfast love endures forever." But the refrain can be as short as an Alleluia or Amen. We find this already in the church of the New Testament where, according to St. Paul, those unskilled in prayer (and singing?) responded with a simple Amen to the person who was leading the prayer (see 1 Cor 14:16).

PRAYER

Almighty and eternal God,
you call us to be one people,
a people who love you
and who love one another.
Fill us with the Spirit of Christ
and assist us as we serve your
assembly's prayer.

"A psalm is the blessing of the people, the praise of God, the commendation of the multitude, the applause of all . . . the voice of the church . . . the joy of liberty, the noise of good cheer, and the echo of gladness." Ambrose of Milan (c.339-397).

Isaiah 66:10-14   Psalm 66:1-3, 4-5, 6-7, 16, 20
Galatians 6:14-18   Luke 10:1-12, 17-20 or 10:1-9

R. *Let all the earth cry out to God with joy.*

Make a joyful noise to God, all the earth;
    sing the glory of his name;
    give to him glorious praise.
Say to God, "How awesome are your deeds!
    Because of your great power, your enemies cringe
        before you."

All the earth worships you;
    they sing praises to you,
    sing praises to your name.
Come and see what God has done;
    he is awesome in his deeds among mortals.

He turned the sea into dry land;
    they passed through the river on foot.
There we rejoiced in him,
    who rules by his might forever.

Come and hear, all you who fear God,
    and I will tell you what he has done for me.
Blessed be God,
    because he has not rejected my prayer
    or removed his steadfast love from me.

Psalm 66 is a psalm of praise and thanksgiving. Perhaps it is composed of what were once two distinct hymns: the first (verses 1-12) being a community hymn, and the second (verses 13-20) being an individual's prayer.

In the first reading Isaiah calls for all people to rejoice: the exile is finally over and peace is returning to Jerusalem. This same joy continues in the psalm: "Shout joyfully . . ."

FOR THE JOURNEY

Again and again the psalms tell us to "sing praise to our God." And indeed this motif of praise permeates our whole liturgy, and especially the eucharistic prayer. We are summoned to be a praise-filled people; we are called to manifest this praise when we gather for worship.

But when we assemble for worship we engage in ritual, a process involving spoken and sung speech, together with symbol, posture, gesture, etc.

Ritual also involves times for silent prayer and reflection, for example, during the penitential rite, after a reading, after the homily, after the presider's "Let us pray," etc.

If our song is to have its full impact, we as singers must join the full assembly in attending to and observing these moments of silence; doing this nourishes and sustains those moments when our voices break out into joyful praise.

RESPONSORIAL PSALM

At an early period the first reading at the liturgy was followed by a psalm. The singer stood on one of the steps (*gradus*) of the reading stand or ambo from which the Scriptures were proclaimed (thus the psalm came to be known as the "gradual").

In time, as the psalm's melody became more ornate, the number of verses was drastically reduced, and the people no longer sang.

In today's liturgy this psalm has been given new life, with the people responding to verses sung by a cantor (or choir). Many commentators see this psalm not so much as a "response" to the first reading, but as a scriptural proclamation, one executed in song by a cantor or choir with the whole assembly joining in the proclamation through the repeated response or antiphon.

PRAYER

Lord God,
source of all goodness and love,
help us to find your word
in poetry, music, painting,
in all that reflects your beauty,
and especially in the silence of our
hearts.

". . . psalmody *listens* even more than it sings." Maurice Zundel, *The Splendour of the Liturgy* (1939)

Fifteenth Sunday of the Year   July 16, 1993

Deuteronomy 30:10-14   Psalm 69:13, 16, 29-30, 32-33, 35, 36
Colossians 1:15-20   Luke 10:25-37

R. *Turn to the Lord in your need, and you will live.*

At an acceptable time, O God,
    in the abundance of your steadfast love, answer me.
With your faithful help rescue me
    from sinking in the mire.
Answer me, O Lord, for your steadfast love is good;
    according to your abundant mercy, turn to me.

But I am lowly and in pain;
    let your salvation, O God, protect me.
I will praise the name of God with a song;
    I will magnify him with thanksgiving

Let the oppressed see it and be glad;
    you who seek God, let your hearts revive.
For the Lord hears the needy,
    and does not despise his own that are in bonds.

For God will save Zion
    and rebuild the cities of Judah;
the children of his servants shall inherit it,
    and those who love his name shall live in it.

This is a psalm of lamentation. The psalmist acknowledges personal misery, disgrace, and guilt; God's assistance is requested. The poem concludes, however, on a more positive note (a later addition?).

The voice of Moses, in the first reading, calls the people to repentance. Salvation and life will be theirs only when they "turn to the Lord in their need." We, for our part, are called to no less.

FOR THE JOURNEY

We all enjoy singing music that is lively and upbeat. It is simply fun to render joyful songs, music that praises God and celebrates the wonders of God.

And yet we are sometimes

called upon to sing a different type of music (for example, during certain seasons of the year or at penitential celebrations). Many psalms, for instance, are known as psalms of lamentation; they tell us that something is wrong in our lives, that things have somehow gone astray.

Music that reflects the downward side of our Christian lives is an important part of our repertoire since it provides a realistic balance in our musical journey toward the day when there will be neither weeping nor sorrow.

ANTIPHONAL SINGING

By antiphonal singing we mean singing in alternating choruses, for example, the singing of successive verses of a psalm by alternating groups of singers.

The word "antiphonal" comes from the Greek "*antiphonia*" (meaning "octave") since in antiquity the 2nd group of singers presumably consisted of boys or women who repeated the melody an octave higher.

St. Ambrose (c.339-397), bishop of Milan, is sometimes credited with introducing antiphonal singing in the west.

PRAYER

Lord God,
you turn sadness into joy,
and tears into rejoicing.
Give us the strength and courage
so that,
as followers of Christ,
we may one day fully share
in the joyful song of your kingdom.

". . . members of the choir also exercise a genuine liturgical function. They ought, therefore, to discharge their office with the sincere piety and decorum demanded by so exalted a ministry and rightly expected of them by God's people. Consequently they must all be deeply imbued with the spirit of the liturgy, each in his own measure, and they must be trained to perform their functions in a correct and orderly manner." Vatican Council II, *Constitution on the Sacred Liturgy* 29.

Genesis 18:1-10   Psalm 15:2-3, 3-4, 5
Colossians 1:24-28   Luke 10:38-42

> R. *He who does justice will live in the presence of the Lord.*
>
> Those who walk blamelessly, and do what is right,
>   and speak the truth from their heart;
> who do not slander with their tongue.
>
> And do no evil to their friends,
>   nor take up a reproach against their neighbors;
> in whose eyes the wicked are despised,
>   but who honor those who fear the Lord
>
> Who do not lend money at interest,
>   and do not take a bribe against the innocent.
> Those who do these things shall never be moved.

Psalm 15 answers a question found in the psalm's opening verse (a verse omitted in the lectionary): "Lord, who shall sojourn in your tent? Who shall dwell on your holy mountain?" The answer is simple: only those possessing certain moral qualities, and especially qualities bearing upon relationships to other people, for example, justice.

Today's reading from Genesis presents the Lord appearing to the patriarch Abraham who extends welcome and hospitality to the three strangers. But the situation is reversed in the psalm. Now it is God who welcomes us, but only when we carry out the works of justice inwardly and outwardly. If we wish to worship God, we must attend to those with whom we share our lives on earth.

FOR THE JOURNEY

In today's second reading Paul says that he, i.e., Paul, became "a minister of [the] church through the commission God gave" him (Col 1:25).

Choir members also minister or serve. But there is something special about the ministry of the choir. A liturgy has only one presider; normally there is only one deacon; a liturgy does not need, for example, two or three acolytes or readers.

But the ministry of the choir is performed by many people who, although coming from diverse backgrounds, act as a single body.

In this the choir is a mirror of the assembly as a whole, since this assembly is made up of many people who gather for one purpose, namely, to praise the Lord. And so the choir not only serves the assembly, but also—in its own way—forms an image of the assembly. And it does so from within the assembly since the choir is part of the people who have gathered to praise God.

ANTIPHON

The term "antiphon" is rather broad, generally referring to a composition or refrain sung in connection with a psalm or canticle.

• The antiphon's text, usually short, is either from Scripture (at times part of the psalm itself) or at times from elsewhere.

• The melody is often simple and syllabic.

The composition supplies a framework for the psalm, often highlighting a particular thought found in one of the psalm verses.

In the Middle Ages the word antiphon was used for certain compositions in honor of the Blessed Virgin, e.g., the *Salve regina*, the *Regina coeli*, etc.

PRAYER

O Lord,
God of wisdom, justice, and love,
make us eager to come into your presence
and worship you.
We are called to minister to your assembly in song;
give us the ability
to do so with faith and dedication.

"There is an appearance of theatrical exhibition in this obtrusive elevation of the singers, who frequently attract the gaze of the congregation (perhaps, I should rather say of the audience) below; who, while the musicians are performing, turn their backs upon minister, altar, and everything sacred, absorbed by that which a savage would actually suppose to be the idol of our worship." William Spark in the *Musical Times* (London) 1853.

Genesis 18:20-32   Psalm 138:1-2, 2-3, 6-7, 7-8
Colossians 2:12-14   Luke 11:1-13

R. *Lord, on the day I called for help, you answered me.*

I give you thanks, O Lord, with my whole heart;
   before the gods I sing your praise;
I bow down toward your holy temple
   and give thanks to your name.

For your steadfast love and your faithfulness;
   for you have exalted your name and your word
     above everything.
On the day I called, you answered me,
   you increased my strength of soul.

For though the Lord is high, he regards the lowly;
   but the haughty he perceives from far away.
Though I walk in the midst of trouble,
   you preserve me against the wrath of my enemies.

You stretch out your right hand,
   and your right hand delivers me.
The Lord will fulfill his purpose for me;
   your steadfast love, O Lord, endures forever.
Do not forsake the work of your hands.

A straightforward hymn of thanksgiving. God has heard the psalmist's prayer, and divine protection will continue.

In Genesis 18:20-32 we read of Abraham entering into dialogue with God over the fate of Sodom. Such a form of prayer requires confidence in God: "When I called, you answered me."

FOR THE JOURNEY

Often we hear a priest presiding at the liturgy say: "Let us begin today's celebration 'In the name of the Father . . .'" Yet this phrasing is not precisely correct. We actually "begin" the liturgy when we join the other members of the assembly in singing the entrance (or gathering) song. This song is a sign of unity and common purpose; furthermore, it often gives the motif of the season or feast being celebrated. In short, it puts us in a suitable frame of mind for sharing at the table of God's word and eucharist.

We must never forget that liturgy is first and foremost the work and activity of the full assembly. It is not only what occurs "up there" at the ambo or at the altar. The Mass, for example, is not "Father's" Mass; it is also "our" Mass. The marriage celebration is not only a celebration by the bride (and groom); it is also and just as importantly a celebration by the whole community.

And so it is important that all our worship celebrations normally begin with all of us joining our voices together in common song, in shared sung prayer.

THE STAFF

Many centuries ago people had to memorize music by rote, but today we have many written aids to assist us as we learn and perform a composition. Among these helps is the staff (or stave), namely, a series of horizontal lines (today they are five in number) upon which musical notes are written, thus indicating the general pitch of the notes.

Historically, the use of such lines had its tentative beginnings in the 9th century. A four line staff was, and continues to be, used in Gregorian Chant.

Our present five line staff appeared about the year 1200.

PRAYER

All faithful God,
hear the prayers of all
who call upon you for help.
Guide us in our journey of life;
may our song
ever echo our faith and trust in you.

"In the celebration of the sacraments it is thus the whole assembly that is leitourgos, each according to his function, but in the 'unity of the Spirit' who acts in all." *Catechism of the Catholic Church* no. 1144.

Daniel 7:9-10, 13-14   Psalm 97:1-2, 5-6, 9
2 Peter 1:16-19   Luke 9:28-36

R. *The Lord is king, the most high over all the earth.*

The Lord is king! Let the earth rejoice;
    let the many coastlands be glad!
Clouds and thick darkness are all around him;
    righteousness and justice are the foundation of
        his throne.

The mountains melt like wax before the Lord,
    before the Lord of all the earth.
The heavens proclaim his righteousness;
    and all the peoples behold his glory.

For you, O Lord, are most high over all the earth;
    you are exalted far above all gods.

Psalm 97, another "kingly psalm," recounts creation's response to the coming of the king and judge of the world.

Daniel's vision is recounted in today's first reading. The prophet saw the "son of man" receiving "dominion, glory, and kingship." Indeed the "Lord is king . . . most high over all the earth."

And the author of 2 Peter testifies that he was present at the transfiguration event; he was an eyewitness and can vouch that Christ is a Lord of "majesty."

Today's feast, which seemingly originated with the dedication of a basilica on Mount Thabor, only entered the west during the 9th and 10th centuries. It was made obligatory by Pope Callistus III (1457) in gratitude for victory over the Turks near Belgrade on August 6, 1456.

FOR THE JOURNEY

There was a time in the history of our worship when music was understood as merely adding a note of solemnity to the ritual. If more solemnity was desired, simply add a deacon and a subdeacon. Or add extra servers. Or have the servers carry lighted candles. Or add a choir, or a larger choir. Music was understood as something external to worship, something akin to frosting on the cake.

Today we are beginning to see that Christian liturgy is, normatively, sung liturgy. A deep union or fundamental relationship exists between liturgy and ritual. When we gather to praise God, our nature calls us to do so in song. As human beings we can do no other than "sing to the Lord." To give praise is, in the words of Charles Wesley (1707-1788), "our duty and our delight."

METER

An essential component of our western music is meter, which has been described as a basic scheme of note values and accents within a composition or section of a composition.

For example, 2/4 meter means that there are two quarter note values within a measure and that the first of these notes is accented.

Musicians speak of simple meter and compound meter.

Examples of *simple* meter are 2/2, 2/4, 2/8 (called duple meter), 3/2, 3/4, 3/8 (called triple meter), and 4/2, 4/4, 4/8 (known as quadruple meter).

Examples of *compound* meter are 6/2, 6/4, 6/8, or 9/4, 9/8, or 12/4, 12/8, 12/16.

PRAYER

Almighty and ever-living God,
help us to proclaim the wonders of
your creation.
Give us the grace of conversion so
that the song on our lips
may ever echo the song in our
hearts.

"Sing lustily and with good courage. Beware of singing as if you are half dead or half asleep, but lift up your voice with strength. Be no more afraid of your voice now, nor more ashamed of its being heard, than when you sing the songs of Satan." John Wesley (1703-1791).

Jeremiah 38:4-6, 8-10   Psalm 40: 1, 2, 3, 17
Hebrews 12:1-4   Luke 12:49-53

R. *Lord, come to my aid!*

I waited patiently for the Lord;
    he inclined to me and heard my cry.

He drew me up from the desolate pit,
        out of the miry bog,
    and set my feet upon a rock,
        making my steps secure.

He put a new song in my mouth,
    a song of praise to our God.
Many will see and fear,
    and put their trust in the Lord.

As for me, I am poor and needy,
    but the Lord takes thought for me.
You are my help and my deliverer;
    do not delay, O my God.

Originally this psalm was two distinct compositions: verses 1-11 being a hymn of thanksgiving; verses 12-18 a plea for help or a lamentation.

Jeremiah is accused and thrown into a well, and yet the Lord saved him. The words of Psalm 40 could well be said by the prophet as a song of thanksgiving: "He drew me up from the desolate pit . . ."

FOR THE JOURNEY

The psalter often speaks of singing a "new song" to the Lord. Our song is to be a "new" song because it signifies a break with the past; there is a fresh direction and orientation.

Unfortunately some voices today are still unable to sing this new song—people who still await the proclamation of the Gospel proclaimed to them, people whom the Gospel message still has to permeate and transform, people whose song reflects not Christ but selfish values.

Our task is not only to sing the new song, but to pray that people everywhere find new life in Christ, that they truly be able to join us in the new song we sing.

ST. PIUS X

Among the popes of the 20th century to whom all of us owe a debt of gratitude is St. Pius X, whose feast is celebrated on August 21st.

Pius X (Giuseppe Sarto) was a parish priest, a seminary professor, the bishop of Mantua, and the cardinal of Venice before being elected pope in 1903.

At a time when people rarely received the eucharist, Pius advocated frequent communion; no less significant was his decision to allow children access to the eucharist. He also reformed the Breviary and reduced the number of saints commemorated in the liturgical calendar.

But Pius X is perhaps most remembered by musicians for his work in restoring Gregorian Chant, especially as a means of promoting the people's "active participation in the holy mysteries and in the public and solemn prayer of the Church."

Pius X is at times quoted as saying "We must not sing or pray during the Mass, but we must sing and pray the Mass." Although the origin of this saying is unknown, it well sums up the thinking of this bold reformer.

PRAYER

Almighty and eternal God,
allow the power of your Spirit
to gather people everywhere
into one family of faith.
May the whole universe
sing your praise forever.

"Sing modestly. Do not bawl, so as to be heard above and distinct from the rest of the congregation—that you may not destroy the harmony—but strive to unite your voices together so as to make one clear melodious sound." John Wesley (1703-1791).

Isaiah 66:19-21   Psalm 117:1, 2
Hebrews 12:5-7, 11-13   Luke 13:22-30

R. *Go out to all the world and tell the Good News.*

Praise the Lord, all you nations!
  Extol him, all you peoples!

For great is his steadfast love toward us,
  and the faithfulness of the Lord endures forever.

This shortest of all the psalms summons people everywhere to praise God because of the Lord's steadfast kindness and enduring faithfulness.

Universality is the theme of today's gospel ("People will come from the east and the west . . ."); Isaiah's message is also one of universality ("I come to gather people of every nation . . ."); and so the whole world is, according to the psalmist, called to "glorify" the Lord.

FOR THE JOURNEY

Paul in today's second reading speaks of discipline and the good fruit it eventually yields.

As singers we well know how important discipline is not only for our lives as Christians (Christ was no cupcake) but also for our musical service to the assembly.

Music making is an enjoyable task, and yet it is a task demanding a sense of responsibility, a honing of skills, and much, much patience. And when a person makes music with other people (as choral singers do) there are even further demands, for example, the discipline of working together with others. No longer is it "my" song; now it is "our" song.

Furthermore, we have to arrange our lives, our schedules, our TV viewing, in order to be present for weekly rehearsals; and during rehearsals we have to focus our attention upon director and music.

At times we might be tempted to waver in our committment, but the words of Paul continue to haunt us: "Lift your drooping hand and strengthen your weak knees . . ." (Heb 12:12).

78

We have all heard that "According to the rubrics, we must . . ." Rubrics are the ceremonial directives for a liturgical service. Since the Middle Ages they have usually been written in red (the Latin *ruber*) to set them off from the prayer texts in the liturgical books.

As liturgical prayers came to be written down, these directives were very sparse. In time their number and volume increased, and they were collected into special booklets called *ordos* or *ordinals*.

Today each liturgical rite is preceded by an introduction or instruction which contains general theological, pastoral, and ceremonial instructions. Presiding ministers and all who share in the preparation of liturgies must read and study these introductions which give so many insights into the ritual action. More specific directions (e.g., "After the silence, one of the following three forms is chosen") are included at appropriate places within the rite itself.

Rubrics are not intended to be directions given by the drill sergeant. They are to be followed respectfully and with intelligence. They link us to how the community prayed yesterday. They give us a framework, a pattern over which we pray today.

PRAYER

God of mercy and love,
help us turn our hearts to you.
May we renew our committment
to you and to your people.
Give us the strength
never to waver
in our service of song.

"Sing in time. Whatever time is sung be sure to keep with it. Do not run before not stay behind it, but attend close to the leading voices, and move therewith as exactly as you can; and take care not to sing too slow. This drawling way naturally steals on us all who are lazy; and it is high time to drive it out from among us, and sing all our tunes just as quick as we did at first." John Wesley (1703-1791).

Twenty-Second Sunday of the Year   September 3, 1995

Sirach 3:17-18, 20, 28-29   Psalm 68:3-4, 5-6, 9-10
Hebrews 12:18-19, 22-24   Luke 14:1, 7-14

R. *God, in your goodness, you have made*
   a home for the poor.

Let the righteous be joyful;
   let them exult before God;
   let them be jubilant with joy.
Sing to God, sing praises to his name.

Father of orphans and protector of widows
   is God in his holy habitation,
God gives the desolate a home to live in;
   he leads out the prisoners to prosperity.

Rain in abundance, O God, you showered abroad;
   you restored your heritage when it
      languished;
your flock found a dwelling in it;
   in your goodness, O God, you provided for
      the needy.

According to some commentators, this psalm, which celebrates God's triumph, was sung while the ark of the covenant was being carried into the temple at Jerusalem.

In today's first reading the prophet reminds us that God cares for the lowly, for those who are in want. The responsorial psalm, in turn, speaks of the God who uses divine power for the benefit of the needy.

FOR THE JOURNEY

Music—like all the arts—can be truly liberating. It can lead us beyond ourselves to an exciting world of tonal colors and hues. Music—again like all the arts—can also be used to enslave and repress . . . we need only think of Hitler's use of song.

As ministers of music we need take care that the songs we sing do not isolate us from the poor, the outcast, the rejected within our society. Our music is not confined to "Alleluia" alone. It is also to be a sign of our efforts to bring about the fullness of God's kingdom in this world.

There must be a connectedness between our ministry as singers and our service on behalf of the marginalized in today's world. "Lord, you have made a home for the poor."

POPE GREGORY

Pope Gregory I (c. 540-604), known as Gregory the Great, was elected pope in 590. An able administrator, a promoter of monasticism, a noted author (his *Liber Regulae Pastoralis* became a classic textbook for bishops in the Middle Ages), Gregory was canonized by acclamation immediately after his death.

Although many authors have long ascribed various liturgical reforms to Gregory, there is no conclusive evidence that the pope codified (much less composed) any of the pieces of plainsong known as Gregorian Chant. In all his writings Gregory never says anything to indicate any interest in music.

Gregory's feast is celebrated on September 3rd.

PRAYER

God our Father,
with you there is neither beginning
nor end.
You love all the creatures of your
hand.
Help us so that the songs we sing
may lead us to do all we can
for those who do not fully share
in the good things of your creation.

"Above all, sing spiritually. Have an eye to God in every word you sing. aim at pleasing Him more than yourself, or any other creature. In order to do this, attend strictly to the sense of what you sing, and see that your heart is not carried away with the sound, but offered to God continually; so shall your singing be such as the Lord will approve here, and reward you when He cometh in the clouds of heaven." John Wesley (1703-1791).

81

Wisdom 9:13-18   Psalm 90:3-4, 5-6, 12-13, 14, 17
Philemon 9-10, 12-17   Luke 14:25-33

R. *In every age, O Lord, you have been our refuge.*

You turn us back to dust,
    and say, "Turn back, you mortals."
For a thousand years in your sight
    are like yesterday when it is past
    or like a watch in the night.

You sweep them away; they are like a dream,
    like grass that is renewed in the morning;
in the morning it flourishes and is renewed;
    in the evening it fades and withers.

So teach us to count our days
    that we may gain a wise heart.
Turn, O Lord! How long?
    Have compassion on your servants.

Satisfy us in the morning with your steadfast love,
    so that we may rejoice and be glad all our days.
Let the favor of the Lord our God be upon us,
    and prosper for us the work of our hands—
    O prosper the work of our hands!

Psalm 90, attributed to Moses, meditates upon the transitory nature of human life. In some monastic circles this psalm was recited each morning as a blessing of the day's work.

To live the life of a disciple of Christ requires the greatest of wisdom, and this wisdom, as the first reading says, comes from God. Our need for wisdom causes us to request: "Teach us to count our days that we may gain a wise heart." It is the Lord and only the Lord who can grant us true wisdom.

FOR THE JOURNEY

Choirs, as we know, are composed of more than a handful of people. By definition a choir is a body of singers, a group of singers—perhaps a large group, perhaps a group of modest numbers.

But one ingrediant of a choir is that its members enhance and support the singing of each other. All the singers, both the seasoned veteran and the most recent recruit, are crucial to the group's efforts. This is indeed an example of where the whole is larger than the sum of its parts.

Never forget that your voice is important . . . your voice is needed. It is *together* that we sing to the Lord.

LITURGICAL COLORS

It was not till the early Middle Ages that rules governing liturgical colors came to be formulated; till this time color was considered less important than the quality and style of the garment's material.

The canons of St. Augustine in Jerusalem prepared the first known sequence of liturgical colors—surprisingly, this schema indicated black for Christmas and for feasts of Our Lady, with blue for the Epiphany and the Ascension.

It was Pope Innocent III (1198-1216) who outlined the Roman schema for liturgical colors: white for feasts, red for martyrs, black for seasons of penance, and green at other times.

Although regional variations (including the use of yellow) long persisted, our present rules for liturgical colors were formally defined by the Missal of Pius V (issued in 1570).

PRAYER

Almighty God,
by the power of your Spirit
help us to sing as one body.
Hear our prayer
so that we might
love and support one another
as we create our song.

"Choirs must be diligently promoted, especially in cathedral churches; but bishops and other pastors of souls must be at pains to ensure that, whenever the sacred action is celebrated with song, the whole body of the faithful may be able to contribute that active participation which is rightly theirs . . . Vatican Council II, *Constitution on the Sacred Liturgy* 114.

Exodus 32:7-11, 13-14   Psalm 51:1-2, 10-11, 15, 17
1 Timothy 1:12-17   Luke 15:1-32 or 15:1-10

R. *I will rise and go to my father.*

Have mercy on me, O God,
    according to your steadfast love;
according to your abundant mercy
    blot out my transgressions.
Wash me thoroughly from my iniquity
    and cleanse me from my sin.

Create in me a clear heart, O God,
    and put a new and right spirit within me.
Do not cast me away from your presence,
    and do not take your holy spirit from me.

O Lord, open my lips,
    and my mouth will declare your praise.
The sacrifice acceptable to God is a broken spirit;
    a broken and contrite heart, O God, you will
        not despise.

Psalm 51 is a penitential psalm proclaiming that sin can indeed be removed, can indeed be "washed away."

God's forgiveness, freely and unreservedly given, appears in all three readings today. And so it is with confidence that we can sing to the Lord, "Have mercy on me . . . thoroughly wash me . . ." Our God is a forgiving God who always takes the first step.

FOR THE JOURNEY

For many centuries—and for a number of reasons—the choir was considered a special group set apart from the people. At one time in history the singers during Mass were thought of a belonging to the clerical state—an ex- tension, as it were, of the clergy at the altar. And for many year, as a result of this, only males (at least according to liturgical law) could be part of this group.

Today we have a completely different perspective. The choir

is considered to be part of the assembly. Ideally, the choir is no longer physically separated from the people, no longer located in a distant loft. When possible, its space is close to the people it serves and of whom it is a part.

Like the prodigal son in today's gospel, we have come home; we have found our true place.

POLYPHONY

By polyphony, from the Greek *"polys"* ("many") and *"phonos"* ("voice"), we mean music having two or more individual part or voices meant to be heard simultaneously.

Polyphony is distinguished from monophony where one part only is sung by one or more voices.

Polyphonic music, which began in the 9th century if not somewhat earlier, flourished during the 16th century. Among the most famous composers of this period are Josquin des Prez (c.1440-1521), Giovanni Pierluigi da Palestrina (1526?-1554), Tomás Luis de Victoria (c.1549-1611), and Lodovico Grossi de Viadana (1564-1645).

Polyphony, together with Gregorian Chant, has long been considered as part of the church's musical patrimony. And yet the demands of today's worship, with its emphasis on the voice of the people and the use of the vernacular, pose a real challenge on how to preserve this musical treasure within today's liturgy.

PRAYER

Father in heaven,
source of unity and love,
may we please you by our
song together.
Help us to be good and faithful
servants
of your holy people.

"The *schola cantorum* or choir exercises its own liturgical function within the assembly. Its task is to ensure that the parts proper to it, in keeping with the different types of chants, are carried out becomingly and to encourage active participation of the people in the singing." *General Instruction of the Roman Missal*, no. 63.

Amos 8:4-7	Psalm 113:1-2, 4-6, 7-8
1 Timothy 2:1-8	Luke 16:1-13 or 16:10-13

> R. *Praise the Lord who lifts up the poor.*
>
> Praise, O servants of the Lord;
>   praise the name of the Lord.
> Blessed be the name of the Lord
>   from this time on and forevermore.
>
> The Lord is high above all nations,
>   and his glory above the heavens.
> Who is like the Lord our God,
>   who is seated on high,
> who looks far down
>   on the heavens and the earth?
>
> He raises the poor from the dust,
>   and lifts the needy from the ash heap,
> to make them sit with princes
>   with the princes of his people.

This hymn of praise, which extolls God who has protected the lowly, the "little people," is prayed during the Jewish family liturgy at Passover.

Money, the things of this earth, concern us today. Jesus says that we serve either money or God. And Amos rebukes those who unjustly exploit the poor, those who show no concern for the needy. And yet, as the psalmist reminds us, God takes special care of the poor, making "them sit with princes, with the princes of his people."

FOR THE JOURNEY

St. Paul in today's second reading speaks of God as desiring that we "come to the knowledge of the truth." For centuries Christianity has felt most comfortable by leading us to God through truths expounded by teachers and preachers . . . by means of rational and intellectual discourse.

On the other hand, the church has usually been wary of visionaries, mystics, and poets as guides on our journey to the divine. Ecclesiastical authorities just seem to have problems coping with those who appeal primarily to the imagination and the heart.

The divine far transcends rational discourse alone, for God's self-revelation is also found in all that is good, beautiful, and enobling on earth—including the gift of music itself. How privileged we are to be part of this discovery.

A CAPPELLA

Most of us know what a choir director means when he or she says that a composition is to be sung "a cappella": it simply means no instrumental accompaniment.

The phrase "a cappella" literally means "in the manner of the chapel," since the liturgical music of such composers as Palestrina (1526?-1594) was performed without musical instruments.

Secular choral music during this period often used instruments, either to double or accompany the voices.

PRAYER

Lord God,
source of all that is good,
give light to our darkness
and joy to our tears.
May the song on our lips
bring our hearts
ever closer to you.

"The psalm which occurred just now in the office blended all voices together, and caused one single fully harmonious chant to arise; young and old, rich and poor, women and men, slaves and free, all sang one single melody . . . All the inequalities of social life are here banished. Together we make up a single choir in perfect equality of rights and of expression whereby earth imitates heaven. Such is the noble character of the Church." John Chrysostom (c.347-407), *Homily 5*.

Amos 6:1, 4-7   Psalm 146:5-7, 8-9, 9-10
1 Timothy 6:11-16   Luke 16:19-31

R. *Praise the Lord, my soul!*

Happy are those whose hope is in the Lord
    their God,
  who keeps faith forever;
who executes justice for the oppressed;
  who gives food to the hungry.
The Lord sets the prisoners free.

The Lord opens the eyes of the blind.
The Lord lifts up those who are bowed down;
  the Lord loves the righteous.

The Lord upholds the orphan and the widow,
  but the way of the wicked he brings to ruin.
The Lord will reign forever,
  your God, O Zion, for all generations.
Praise the Lord!

This hymn extolling God's kindness and generosity is the first of the "Halleluiah Psalms" (Psalms 146-150) which conclude the psalter.

Similar to last Sunday, today's gospel and Old Testament readings concern the rich and the poor. Amos rebukes the rich and powerful. God, on the other hand, frees, feeds, sustains, and raises up all who live at society's margins.

FOR THE JOURNEY

When we "praise the Lord," most of us prefer to do so by singing in parts. Singing in harmony is fun to do, challenging, and quite satisfying. When asked to sing in unison, we might be tempted to look down upon such an "elementary" choral form.

Nonetheless, unison singing has a special and honored place in the history of sung liturgy, and for a reason. Unison singing gathers together many people and forms their voices into one melody—all sing with a single voice.

When we sing in unison, we manifest that unity which is a hallmark of the assembly and the church. We are one both in spirit and in voice.

ENTRANCE SONG

Beginnings are important. And this is especially true when we gather for worship. It is no accident that the church's tradition is to begin its liturgy with song, a song which accompanies the ministers as they process into the church.

In Rome the singers chanted a psalm text which began and concluded with a short antiphon. But as the music became more elaborate and as the procession came to be abbreviated, the piece was reduced to the antiphon, one psalm verse, the doxology, and the repetition of the psalm verse.

Today great freedom is allowed in selecting the text. And the whole assembly generally participates in this song whose purpose is, in the words of the missal, "to open the celebration, deepen the unity of the people, introduce them to the mystery of the feast or season, and accompany the procession (GI 25).

PRAYER

Almighty God,
Creator of all things,
you alone are the source
of all unity.
Help us as we sing
so that our song may flow
from voices united
in faith and in love.

"Our voice ought not to be dissonant but consonant. One ought not to drag out the singing while another cuts it short, and one ought not to sing too low while another raises his voice. Rather, each should strive to integrate his voice within the sound of the harmonious chorus . . ." Niceta of Remesiana (d. after 414).

Habakkuk 1:2-3; 2:2-4   Psalm 95:1-2, 6-7, 8-9
2 Timothy 1:6-8, 13-14   Luke 17:5-10

R. *If today you hear his voice, harden not your hearts.*

O come, let us sing to the Lord;
  let us make a joyful noise to the rock of our salvation.
Let us come into his presence with thanksgiving
  let us make a joyful noise to him with songs of praise!

O come, let us worship and bow down,
  let us kneel before the Lord, our Maker!
For he is our God,
  and we are the people of his pasture,
  and the sheep of his hand.

O that today you would listen to his voice!
  Do not harden your hearts, as at Meribah,
  as on the day at Massah in the wilderness
    when your ancestors tested me,
  and put me to the proof, though they had seen my
    work.

In this psalm, which long introduced the hour of matins in the Roman Breviary, the people are invited to praise and worship the Lord, our Maker.

Today's readings stress the gift of faith; and yet faith does not exist in a vacuum; we know that God protects us since "we are the people he shepherds, the flock he guides." For our part, we must keep our ears open to God's word, and our hearts open to its message.

FOR THE JOURNEY

Have you ever noticed how people sing so naturally at birthday parties? Or on New Year's Eve? Or at charismatic gatherings? Or even on July Fourth as they join in "God Bless America"?

Those who study this phenomenon tell us that singing comes naturally to people who have something to sing about, when events or memories so move the heart that vocal expression automatically results.

In today's gospel Jesus stresses the importance of faith in the lives of his apostles. Our song, if it is to be a Christian song, must reflect and flow from our faith in Christ and his message. We must be faith-filled singers.

CHORALE

Strictly speaking, a "chorale" is a hymn *tune* of the German Evangelical Church. Broadly speaking, the term denotes both the text and melody of German hymns, especially those of the Protestant Reformation.

Although the German people sang vernacular hymns well before the Reformation, it was Martin Luther (1483-1546) who became the father of evangelical hymnody. He considered the chorale as an important foundation for his religious work.

Chorale texts came from many sources, including Latin hymns and folk song materials. Secular melodies were at times given religious texts; and new compositions were written.

Recent evolution in Catholic hymnals has witnessed many German chorale melodies and texts being sung during the Roman liturgy.

PRAYER

Almighty and all-powerful God,
you strengthen and protect
all who call upon you.
Pour out your blessings among us
so that the praises we sing
may flow from hearts that are
strong in faith
and filled with love.

"A person who gives this some thought and yet does not regard it [music] as a marvelous creation of God, must be a clodhopper indeed and does not deserve to be called a human being; he should be permitted to hear nothing but the braying of asses and the grunting of hogs." Martin Luther (1483-1546).

2 Kings 5:14-17   Psalm 98:1, 2-3, 3-4
2 Timothy 2:8-13   Luke 17:11-19

R. *The Lord has revealed to the nations his saving power.*

O sing to the Lord a new song,
   for he has done marvelous things.
His right hand and his holy arm
   have gotten him victory.

The Lord has made known his victory;
   he has revealed his vindication in the sight of the
     nations.
He has remembered his steadfast love and faithfulness
   to the house of Israel.

All the ends of the earth have seen
   the victory of our God.
Make a joyful noise to the Lord, all the earth;
   break forth into joyous song and sing praises.

The psalmist sings in praise of the Lord who is king. All nature, indeed the whole world, is to acclaim the Lord.

Gratitude is a precious human quality. And the foundation of our gratitude is that God has worked wonders throughout human history. Just as Jesus, in today's gospel, cured the ten lepers, so he continues to do "wondrous deeds," making salvation known "to the nations."

FOR THE JOURNEY

One of the distinguishing characteristics of both Judaism and Christianity is that God is not a far distant, remote deity, but a God who dwells among us, a God who is at work in creation, a God who assumes an active role in human history, both past and present. God has indeed "revealed his power," and continues to do so.

Praise and thanksgiving encapsulate our response to God's deeds. Aware of what God has accomplished, of what God still accomplishes, we can merely marvel and utter our wonder and admiration. By so doing we become fully human.

And our praise, when expressed in song, is raised to a new height; it involves our whole person. Our whole body—with its physical, affective, and mental dimensions—becomes an instrument giving glory to God.

BELLS

Church bells have existed from the earliest centuries of Christianity. Originally they were carried in the hand and struck with a mallet. But by the 6th century they were fixed to buildings, and from the 9th century on hung in towers. First used in monasteries, the popularity of bells soon spread to parish churches.

Throughout history bells have served a variety of purposes: as a sign of joy ("to ring in a feast") and of sadness (the death bell); to mark parts of the liturgy and to indicate times for prayer (the morning, noon, and evening *Angelus*).

In the Middle Ages it was customary to "baptize" bells with salt water and to anoint them—people believed the tolling of the bell would protect the church from storms and drive away the evil spirits.

Today church bells are blessed, sprinkled with holy water, and incensed. "The peal of bells . . . is in a way the expression of the sentiments of the people of God as they rejoice or grieve, offer thanks or petition, gather together and show outwardly the mystery of their oneness in Christ" (*Book of Blessings* 1305).

PRAYER

Lord God,
you indeed touch our lives
with your mercy and grace.
Help us to praise you
with all our being,
to worship you
in spirit and in truth.

"The aim and final reason for all music should be nothing else but the glory of God and the refreshment of the spirit." J.S. Bach (1684-1750).

Twenty-Ninth Sunday of the Year   October 22, 1995

Exodus 17:8-13   Psalm 121:1-2, 3-4, 5-6, 7-8
2 Timothy 3:14-4:2   Luke 18:1-8

R. *Our help is from the Lord*
  who made heaven and earth.

I lift up my eyes to the hills—
  from where will my help come?
My help comes from the Lord,
  who made heaven and earth.

He will not let your foot be moved;
  he who keeps you will not slumber.
He who keeps Israel
  will neither slumber nor sleep.

The Lord is your keeper;
  the Lord is your shade at your right hand.
The sun shall not strike you by day,
  nor the moon by night.

The Lord will keep you from all evil;
  he will keep your life.
The Lord will keep
  your going out and your coming in
  from this time on and forevermore.

The psalmist, confident of God's assistance, assures others of divine protection.

Faithful perseverence in prayer is a motif of today's first and third readings. Such prayer was practiced by the psalmist who truly experienced that "help comes from the Lord."

FOR THE JOURNEY

Paul, writing to Timothy, insists upon the importance of sacred Scripture. We are told that Scripture must be respected and preached; God's word is an inspired word and profits our sal-

94

vation. It is axiomatic that the divine word holds a privileged position within the church and within the liturgy.

Thus language itself is an element of our worship. Words, often formal in style, are repeated, listened to, memorized. Whether the words are spoken or sung, they are an important vehicle of communication. They exist to be understood.

All choral music (and this includes choral music sung as part of the liturgy) combines two art forms: poetry and music. Our everyday lethargic speech patterns, unless corrected in rehearsal, simply mar the beauty of choral singing.

Thus wise choir directors do not overlook the demands of enunciation, pronunciation, diction, and phrasing. Dry technique, perhps. But crucial to the artistic and prayerful quality of our song.

ORDINARY OF THE MASS

Choir directors often refer to the "Ordinary of the Mass." This expression, which is somewhat dated and used less and less frequently today, designates those texts generally common to all Masses.

Included in the Ordinary would be, for example, the eucharistic prayer, the Lord's Prayer, greetings, dialogues, etc.

Among the chants of the Ordinary would be the *Kyrie eleison* (penitential rite), the Glory to God, the Holy Holy, and the Lamb of God.

PRAYER

All-powerful God,
by the power of your word
you lead us
to the fullness of truth.
May the words we sing
call to mind
your goodness, mercy, and love.

"While your tongue sings, let your mind seek out the meaning of the words, so that you might sing in spirit and sing also in understanding." Basil the Great (c.330-379).

Sirach 35:12-14, 16-18   Psalm 34:1-2, 16-17, 18, 22
2 Timothy 4:6-8, 16-18   Luke 18:9-14

R. *The Lord hears the cry of the poor.*

I will bless the Lord at all times;
    his praise shall continually be in my mouth.
My soul makes its boast in the Lord;
    let the humble hear and be glad.

The face of the Lord is against evildoers,
    to cut off the remembrance of them from the earth.
When the righteous cry for help, the Lord hears,
    and rescues them from all their troubles.

The Lord is near to the brokenhearted,
    and saves the crushed in spirit.
the Lord redeems the life of his servants;
    none of those who take refuge in him will be condemned.

This psalm is also used on the Fourth Sunday of Lent, Cycle C.

In today's gospel Jesus tells us that the tax collector was justified by his humble prayer. And, as our reading from Sirach recalls, God takes special care of the powerless, the needy. We are called to bless the Lord who "hears the cry of the poor." God hears the cry of the humble, those who replace self-sufficiency with generous service.

FOR THE JOURNEY

To "bless the Lord at all times" means that our prayer is to be continuous; it concerns an attitude toward God that is to last throughout life. It is to find God in all that we do as Christians.

As singers are we not also called to "sing to the Lord at all times"? Should not God's melody continuously resound in our hearts and souls?

Should we not see God's

beauty in all that is good, and listen to God's voice not only within us, but also in the song of the birds, the rustle of the wind, the murmuring of the brook, and the stillness of a summer evening?

PREFACE

Contrary to our common understanding of the word, the "preface" in the Mass does not mean an introduction to something.

The preface (which itself begins with the dialogue between the presiding priest and the assembly) is the opening section of the eucharistic prayer. Although the whole of this prayer is one of thanks and praise, the motives for such are principally expressed in the preface. Praise is given not only because of God's greatness and majesty, but also because of the wonders God has accomplished on our behalf. Through divine power we have been created, redeemed, and sanctified.

In the early centuries of the church there were many prefaces; the Roman liturgy gradually reduced their number; and yet today, as the result of Vatican II's liturgical reform, our missal has over 80 preface texts.

It is interesting to note that the opening dialogue of the preface is mirrored, as it were, by the people's "Amen" concluding the eucharistic prayer. This prayer is proclaimed on behalf of all the gathered people. Through baptism all share in the priesthood of Christ.

PRAYER

Almighty God,
Lord of the universe,
open the eyes of our hearts
so that we may continuously find
your goodness and beauty
in all that you have created
for our enjoyment.

"Throughout our entire lives, then, we celebrate a feast, persuaded that God is present everywhere and in all things: we plough the fields while giving praise, we sail the seas while singing hymns . . ." Clement of Alexandria (c.150-c.215).

97

Wisdom 11:22-12:1   Psalm 145:1-2, 8-9, 10-11, 13, 14
2 Thessalonians 1:11-2:2   Luke 19:1-10

R. I will praise your name for ever, my king and my God.

I will extol you, my God and King,
   and bless your name forever and ever.
Every day I will bless you,
   and praise your name forever and ever.

The Lord is gracious and merciful,
   slow to anger and abounding in steadfast love.
The Lord is good to all,
   and his compassion is over all that he has made.

All your works shall give thanks to you, O Lord,
   and all your faithful shall bless you.
They shall speak of the glory of your kingdom,
   and tell of your power.

The Lord is faithful in all his words,
   and gracious in all his deeds.
The Lord upholds all who are failing,
   and raises up all who are bowed down.

This psalm is also used on the 5th Sunday of Easter in Cycle C.

Luke's Gospel presents Our Lord entering the house of a sinner, Zacchaeus; and the Book of Wisdom speaks of God having mercy on all and overlooking our sins. Yes, God's mercy and forgiveness is universal; the all-powerful God is "gracious and merciful" to all.

FOR THE JOURNEY

Rituals, with their repeated patterns of action, offer us security. They give us familiar ways of doing things . . . we always know what's coming next—like dance patterns performed over and over again.

Much music is similar to this: the hymns and other songs we sing repeatedly year after year.

Musically, these pieces help us feel "at home"; they create a climate of customariness and calmness. They are long-standing musical friends.

But at times we are called upon to sing music that might surprise or disturb us: unfamiliar rhythms, unusual melodies, unexpected harmonies, and the like. Such pieces can distance us from what is routine and ordinary.

But at the same time they can open us up to God's presence in the unknown, in the unfamiliar, in mystery. Indeed all God's works can reveal the divine presence.

DOXOLOGY

One of the textual components of our Christian liturgy is a form of prayer called a "doxology." A doxology (from the Greek "*doxa*" [glory] and "*logos*" [word] is a text of praise—usually praise of the Trinity.

Here are some examples of doxologies in the Roman liturgy:

• the "Glory to God in the Highest . . ." (called the greater doxology);
• the "Glory be to the Father and to the Son . . ." (called the lesser doxology);
• the "Through him, with him . . ." at the conclusion of the eucharistic prayer;
• the final stanza of many hymns.

PRAYER

Almighty God,
your goodness and beauty
are the foundation
of our song of praise.
Embrace us with your loving grace
so that we may ever be open
to the wonders
you have prepared for us.

"Music should be pleasant, gay, uplifting, enjoyable, if it is to fulfill its destiny . . . Like most rare and precious things, the exquisite quality of a work is not be to discerned all at once. It must be discovered." Nadia Boulanger (1887-1979).

2 Maccabees 7:1-2, 9-14   Psalm 17:1, 5-6, 8, 15
2 Thessalonians 2:16-3:5   Luke 20:27-38 or 20:27, 34-38

R. *Lord, when your glory appears, my joy will be full.*

Hear a just cause, O Lord; attend to my cry;
   give ear to my prayer from lips free of deceit.

My steps have held fast to your paths;
   my feet have not slipped.
I call upon you, for you will answer me, O God;
   incline your ear to me, hear my words.

Guard me as the apple of the eye;
   hide me in the shadow of your wings.
I shall behold your face in righteousness;
   when I awake I shall be satisfied, beholding your
      presence.

Psalm 17 is a declaration that the psalmist has been faithful to the Lord.

Today's readings concern faith, especially faith in the resurrection (1st and 3rd readings). God can indeed raise people from the dead (1st reading); and Jesus tells the Sadducees that they do not understand what will happen as the result of the resurrection. On the day of the resurrection the Lord's glory will appear—it will be a day on which our "joy will be full."

FOR THE JOURNEY

It has often been said that the liturgy as reformed by Vatican II requires much more of its ministers than did the church's worship prior to the council. Our liturgy today is more transparent; ministers must put more of themselves into it.

The way ministers "look," the way they carry out their tasks impacts ever so much on creating a visual environment for prayer.

The same is true for those of us who are liturgical singers. The way we stand and sit, the way we hold our music, the way we focus

100

attention upon the director—our whole collective visual appearance says ever so much about ourselves; it strengthens or weakens the assembly's ability to pray.

AMEN

How often in the liturgy we sing "Amen." This Hebrew word, found in both the Old and New Testaments, means "verily" or "so be it."

Following synagogue usage, the word was quickly adopted by the early church (see 1 Cor 14:16), especially as a verbal sign that the people confirmed or assented to a prayer.

The most important Amen in our liturgy today occurs at the conclusion of the eucharistic prayer when the whole assembly sings out that it assents to this prayer of praise and thanksgiving.

Composers of the 17th and 18th centuries took great delight in repeating this word over and over again; for example, in Cherubini's D Minor Mass the sopranos repeat the Amen 107 times at the end of the Creed.

PRAYER

Lord God,
you constantly reveal
your glory to us
through the miracles of creation.
We ask that your Spirit
guide our voices
as we sing of your
wonderful works.

"The choir, cock and hen variety, were in the habit of cracking and eating nuts during the service, which did not improve the naturally harsh Suffolk voices, and the shells were left week after week on the floor, in spite of the dustpan and brush, kept for convenience under the altar." Dorothy Thompson, in *Sophia's Son*, describing the installation of her father as rector in Aldeburgh, Suffolk, in 1874.

Malachi 3:19-20   Psalm 98:5-6, 7-8, 9
2 Thessalonians 3:7-12   Luke 21:5-19

> R. *The Lord comes to rule the earth with justice.*
>
> Sing praises to the Lord with the lyre,
>   with the lyre and the sound of melody.
> With trumpets and the sound of the horn
>   make a joyful noise before the King, the Lord.
>
> Let the sea roar, and all that fills it;
>   the world and those who live in it.
> Let the floods clap their hands;
>   let the hills sing together for joy.
>
> At the presence of the Lord, for he is coming
>   to judge the earth.
> He will judge the world with righteousness,
>   and the peoples with equity.

This psalm (though with different verses) is also used on the 28th Sunday of the Year in Cycle C.

As the liturgical year is approaching its conclusion, the church looks forward to the last times. In the words of Malachi, the "sun of justice" will arise on the day of the Lord. It will be a time when, according to today's psalm, the Lord "will judge the world with righteousness." It will be a time of perfect justice.

Year after year we hear the Scriptures telling us of the approaching Day of the Lord. The Reign of God is at hand. Each age must confront the seriousness of the times. Christ is coming, and what he has prepared for us defies human imagination.

FOR THE JOURNEY

The focal point of a choir's activity is the Sunday assembly, the people called by God to gather together for worship. The assembly we serve gathers in a particular church building and at a particular time.

Yet this assembly (and its song) has another dimension. What we do on earth prefigures and is a sign of what will be happening on the last day. Our earthly liturgy anticipates that of tomorrow.

As wonderful as our choral prayer of praise may now be, all the more magnificent will it be on the Day of the Lord. What we now do only after hours of practice, we will then accomplish naturally, without effort. Never has the world experienced the singing of such a choir.

ST. CAECILIA

On November 22nd we will celebrate the feast of St. Caecilia, the patroness of musicians.

In the early church Caecilia was highly venerated as a virgin (she remained so even after her marriage) and also as a martyr. In fact, her name is mentioned in the Roman Canon of the Mass.

Already in the 4th century a church in Caecilia's honor was erected in Rome, on the site where her house once stood; and in the following century a rather fanciful account of her martyrdom was written.

Caecilia's relics were discovered in the catacomb of Praetextatus by Paschal I (817-824), and moved to her church. When the church was remodeled in 1599, her grave was opened and her body was found incorrupt.

PRAYER

Lord God,
the day is coming
when we will see you
face to face.
Fill us with hope and joy
so that our voices
may ever sing
of the fullness of your kingdom.

"Singing fashions a community, as the harmony of voices fosters the harmony of hearts. It eliminates differences of age, origin, and social class and it brings everyone into one accord in praising God." Paul VI (24 September 1972).

2 Samuel 5:1-3   Psalm 122:1-2, 3-4, 4-5
Colossians 1:12-20   Luke 23:35-43

R. *I rejoiced when I heard them say:*
   let us go to the house of the Lord.

I was glad when they said to me,
   "Let us go to the house of the Lord!"
Our feet are standing
   within your gates, O Jerusalem.

Jerusalem—built as a city
   that is bound firmly together.
To it the tribes go up,
   the tribes of the Lord.

As was decreed for Israel,
   to give thanks to the name of the Lord.
For there the thrones for judgment were set up,
   the thrones of the house of David.

A pilgrimage song. As the travellers approach Jerusalem, the psalmist extols the Holy City. Jerusalem is the home not only of the chosen people; it is also the place where God is present to the people. In short, Jerusalem is the city of God, the earthly symbol of the coming of God's kingdom.

FOR THE JOURNEY

We often refer to Christ as teacher, preacher, prophet, healer, priest, and king.

This kingship of Christ will be especially apparent on the Last Day when the fullness of the kingdom will be inaugurated. The Scriptures use various im-ages to portray this spectacle which will stun the eyes and enthrall the ears. In fact, the biblical authors seem to stretch our powers of imagination as they picture the wonders of this day.

May we not even believe that when Christ comes he will come

as a singer, inviting us to join in a melodious refrain which embraces the heavens and the earth, transcends human time, and continues into eternity?

_____ ST. CAECILIA, PATRONESS OF MUSICIANS _____

The account of Caecilia's martyrdom relates that Caecilia, in the midst of the profane instrumental music played at her wedding, sang in her heart ("*in corde suo*") to God.

When the first antiphon for Laudes (an hour of the Divine Office) was composed, the author used the text from the martyrdom account but simply omitted "*in corde suo*"—giving the impression that Caecilia was actually singing to God.

Starting as early as the 8th century, representations appear of Caecilia, either actually playing the organ or sitting before an instrument (organ or harp) while singing.

Thus it appears that Caecilia's connection with music has a liturgical origin.

And in case the members of your choir forgot to hold a celebration in honor of St. Caecilia last Wednesday—remember, it's never to late to have a party.

PRAYER

Lord God,
you have created us
so that we might
image your beauty and power.
Send your Spirit upon us
so that our souls may give you thanks,
our hearts may love you,
and our voices sing your praise.

"Apart from those moment when the Scriptures are being read or a sermon is preached, when the bishop is praying aloud or the deacon is specifying the intentions of the litany of community prayer, is there any time when the faithful assembled in the church are not singing? Truly I see nothing better, more useful or more holy that they could do." Augustine (354-430), *Letter 55*.